CONTENTS

Tank Battles of World War Two

4 Armour in World War Two
6 Tank Warfare
10 Early War Tanks 1939–42
14 Late War Tanks 1943–45
18 Armoured Fighting Vehicles
20 Anti-Tank Weapons
22 Matilda II
23 Cromwell
24 M4 Sherman
25 Tiger
26 Panther
27 T-34
28 Captured Tanks
32 Cadet Orlik in Poland, 1939
36 Panzer versus Char at Stonne
40 The Battle of Arras
44 Beda Fomm
48 Easter Victory at Tobruk
52 Battle of Dubno June 1941
56 Outpost Snipe
60 The B Company Offensive
64 The Battle of Happy Valley

68 Captain Hollands' One-Tank Offensive
72 Panzer Killers at El Guettar
76 Kursk
80 Panzer IVs and T-34s
84 Operation Goodwood
88 Killing Michael Wittman

92 Arracourt
96 Tank Battle on Christmas Eve
100 Drive to Bastogne
104 The Sherman in Soviet Service
108 Pershing versus Panther
112 Afterward
114 Glossary and Terms

LEFT: A smoking Panther tank seen through the driver's hatch of a Soviet SU-85 assault gun. The 85mm gun was effective against the Panther's armour within around 500m. (SOVIET ARCHIVES)

LEFT: A classic image of a Panzer III with German infantry on the Eastern Front in mid-1941. By this time most Panzer IIIs carried a 50mm cannon but still had trouble against the Soviet T-34. (AUSTRALIAN WAR MEMORIAL)

COVER PHOTO: The crew of the Pershing tank 'Eagle 7' after their duel with Oberleutnant Bartelborth's Panther in Cologne in March 1945. (US ARMY)

ISBN: 978 1 80282 006 7
Editor: Chris Miskimon
Senior editor, specials: Roger Mortimer
Email: roger.mortimer@keypublishing.com
Cover design: Steve Donovan
Cover colouration: colourbyrjm.co.uk
Design: SJmagic DESIGN SERVICES, India
Advertising Sales Manager: Brodie Baxter
Email: brodie.baxter@keypublishing.com
Tel: 01780 755131
Advertising Production: Becky Antoniades
Email: Rebecca.antoniades@keypublishing.com

SUBSCRIPTION/MAIL ORDER
Key Publishing Ltd, PO Box 300,
Stamford, Lincs, PE9 1NA
Tel: 01780 480404
Subscriptions email:
subs@keypublishing.com
Mail Order email:
orders@keypublishing.com
Website: www.keypublishing.com/shop

PUBLISHING
Group CEO and Publisher: Adrian Cox

Published by
Key Publishing Ltd, PO Box 100,
Stamford, Lincs, PE9 1XQ
Tel: 01780 755131
Website: www.keypublishing.com

PRINTING
Precision Colour Printing Ltd, Haldane,
Halesfield 1, Telford, Shropshire. TF7 4QQ

DISTRIBUTION
Seymour Distribution Ltd, 2 Poultry Avenue,
London, EC1A 9PU
Enquiries Line: 02074 294000.

Armour in World War Two

Tanks appeared in World War One as an answer to the stalemate of trench warfare. While their use saw some success, technological shortcomings and immature tactics limited what could be accomplished. Had the war continued into 1919, tanks would have played a large role in the planned Allied offensive. The tank's promise as a decisive weapon was apparent to a few visionaries who refined and developed tank design over the next two decades.

As a result, tanks became a primary weapon in World War Two, produced in huge numbers and used in every theatre of operations by all the major armies. Tactics and theory matured throughout the war in the harsh crucible of combat. In this special edition we will examine the tank during the war, when it truly came of age as a fully functional weapon system. This is when designers, planners, leaders and tank crews learned to create and use battleworthy tanks to their greatest potential.

One of the most important lessons of armoured warfare is to see the tank not as a standalone weapon system, but as one piece of an integrated mechanised unit. Even in groups, tanks are actually very vulnerable

when operating alone. They are most effective when used as part of a well-coordinated combined arms force. Combined arms doctrine uses armour, infantry, artillery, engineers and air support together in mutually supporting ways.

Tanks excel at smashing through enemy defences and penetrating into their rear areas to cause havoc. Engineers destroy enemy obstacles and clear lanes through minefields for the tanks to advance. Artillery and air support pave the way for the armour's breakthrough by bombardments and airstrikes. Infantry must be able to

keep pace with the armour as they are mutually supporting. Infantry protect tanks from enemy anti-tank guns and enemy troops armed with handheld anti-tank weapons. The tanks provide gunfire support to infantry with their cannon and machine guns, suppressing or destroying enemy defensive positions such as bunkers and machine gun nests. Friendly tanks also keep enemy tanks at a distance.

During the war's early years all nations struggled to make combined arms operations work effectively. The Germans did so most effectively as

they had made the most progress in perfecting such techniques before the war. War is complex, however, and even they had difficulty making it all work. During early campaigns the panzers frequently outran their supporting infantry, who did not have enough halftracks or lorries to keep up. German panzer units often had to stop to wait for the infantry to catch up.

The Germans got better over time, but so did everyone else. The British, American and Soviet armies all had to learn the same lessons while catching up to their foe. Once they did, they began to make better progress. By the end of the war the Allies were well able to coordinate large, well-supported armoured attacks.

Armoured warfare, then, is more than just duels between tanks. In these pages you will read accounts of tank crews in battle, anti-tank units in defence and offence and see the battlefield from the commander's eye down to the view of individual tank crews in the stress of battle. In a few cases, duels did occur, and we have a few of those tales as well.

In this edition, we have focused on the European and North African theatres, as this is where the bulk of armoured warfare took place. Wherever possible, photographs of the battles in question are used to show the reader what the combatants experienced. Camera quality being what it was at the time, please excuse the occasional blurry or poorly lit image; keep in mind those who took them were under fire at the time!

**Christopher Miskimon
Major, Field Artillery, USA (Ret.)
Editor**

ABOVE: A joint British-American tank force prepares for an attack on Brachelen, Germany. The Churchill and Shermans are camouflaged with a combination of whitewash and white cloth sheets (US NATIONAL ARCHIVES)

LEFT: A Panzer II of the 18th Panzer Division crossing a river in Russia in 1941. This division's panzers were equipped for submersible operations, originally intended for the invasion of England. (AUSTRALIAN WAR MEMORIAL)

Tank Warfare

Employing and destroying armoured vehicles

ABOVE: The Red Army used their own designs and lend-lease tanks from the US and UK. Here a Soviet Sherman and T-34/85 link up with American forces on 2 May 1945 near Linz, Austria. (US NATIONAL ARCHIVES)

The various combatants entered World War Two using a variety of tanks, designed mostly on theory and limited experience. The budgetary restrictions of the 1920s and 30s curtailed experimentation while technological barriers limited size, weight, protection and armament. The horrors of World War One still loomed heavily in the minds of many, further curbing interest in developing new weapons.

This meant everyone brought their best ideas about how to build and employ tanks to war in 1939-41. Those concepts varied widely, from massed combined arms operations to the use of tanks in small groups for infantry support. Sometimes tanks were used almost as horse cavalry of the previous century, making unsupported charges.

The Germans quickly demonstrated the effectiveness of their combined arms tactics. Often known as '*blitzkrieg*,' or 'lightning war,' the Germans thought of it more as '*bewegungskrieg*,' or 'war of movement.' It was not so much a new way of

RIGHT: The M3 medium tank in its two variants, the Lee and the Grant, served as a stopgap design in North Africa due to shortages of the M4 Sherman. Its 75mm gun had a good high-explosive round. (US NATIONAL ARCHIVES)

fighting as a way to use modern technology such as armoured vehicles, radio, and airpower in a coordinated fashion alongside infantry and artillery.

The primary advantage of the German ground forces in the campaigns of 1939-41 lay in their ability to coordinate rapid movements. This came about partly through training and partly through innovative use of new technology. For example, in France in 1940 and the Soviet Union in Summer 1941, the French and Soviet Armies had more tanks and many of those tanks were better armed and armoured than their German counterparts. They were beginning to form dedicated armoured units but many of their tanks were distributed in small numbers for infantry support.

Once combat began, at the operational level the French did not concentrate their forces quickly enough to counter rapid German thrusts. It took time to bring tanks together, refuel them and prepare them for action while German artillery and dive-bombers struck at them. The French and Soviet troops fought bravely but were unable to match the German pace.

At the tactical level, German tanks held several key advantages which compensated for their often-weaker armament and protection. The German Panzer III and IV had larger turrets to accommodate a gunner and loader as well as the commander, allowing the commander to concentrate fully on battlefield awareness. In many Allied tanks, the commander also acted as the gunner, which distracted from leading the tank. This was only a partial advantage as many of the tanks Germany used in the invasions of

1940-41 were older models with the same shortcoming.

A great advantage lay in the panzer force's widespread issue of radios. German armoured units could coordinate their movements and attacks over significant distances. Many Allied units only had radios

installed in platoon and company leader's vehicles. This meant the rest of the unit had to stay close to the leader to watch for hand or flag signals or perhaps flares. Even so, the smoke and dust raised in battle often obscured signalling, causing confusion. Tanks bunched around a leader also made easier targets. On the Eastern Front, for example, German gunners soon learned how to spot the enemy leader's tank by how it moved and led the tanks around it.

The initial advantages the Germans enjoyed established their reputation, but their opponents learned through the harsh test of combat. The Americans did not enter combat against the Germans until late 1942, learning their lessons in North Africa. By mid-1944 the Allies were able to launch well-coordinated combined arms assaults of their own. Meanwhile, the Germans, losing the war of attrition, over time became less able to mount effective armoured attacks.

While senior leaders and staffs perfected the art of combined arms warfare, on the battlefield, tank crews lived with their tanks. When not on operations, tanks had to be

ABOVE: Tank Crews spend hours cleaning and maintaining their tanks. This crew, from 16/5 Lancers, clean the barrel of the six-pounder gun on their Crusader tank in Tunisia, 1943. (IWM TR939)

LEFT: German tank destroyers were vulnerable to flanking fire; this Jagdpanther, on display at the Imperial War Museum in London, has four shot penetrations in it right side. (AUTHOR)

ABOVE: A Soviet T-34 during a night attack, January 1944. Though the image is likely posed, it shows close coordination of tanks and infantry.
(SOVIET ARCHIVES)

BELOW: American military police inspect a mock-up of a T-34 at a captured German base in 1945. It was used for anti-tank training of German recruits.
(US NATIONAL ARCHIVES)

refuelled, rearmed ('bombed up') and constantly maintained. Even the most reliable tank designs would soon fail in the field without daily checks and upkeep.

In action, tank crews spent most of their time supporting infantry and firing at bunkers, machine gun nests, artillery observers and similar enemy positions. Reflecting this, a tank's ammunition racks usually carried more high explosive and smoke rounds than armour-piercing shot. Tank versus tank combat occurred rarely. The tank's main enemy in World War Two was the anti-tank gun, though tanks were often lost to mines, artillery, aircraft and handheld anti-tank weapons like the panzerfaust and bazooka.

Enemy tanks were a major cause of fear in tank crews, however. Several German generals noted after the war that German tank crews most feared allied tanks and tank destroyers; they also noted their greatest tank losses were suffered through mechanical breakdown on the way to the battle! Interviews with German tank crews noted they particularly feared the white phosphorus rounds allied tankers often used against them. This round could blind the crew, set fire to the tank or at least make the crew think their vehicle was on fire and abandon it.

Conversely, Allied tankers feared German tanks as well. For American crews, the fear of encountering a Tiger

LEFT: A Panzer III moves past a shattered Soviet T-28 tank in August 1941. It was likely hit by a large-calibre artillery piece or suffered an ammunition explosion. (POLISH ARCHIVES)

proved pervasive. Observers often misidentified any German tank as a Tiger; this was made worse by many American troops using the name Tiger as a nickname for any German armoured vehicle.

When tank against tank actions did occur, success often came down to whoever spotted the enemy armour first, fired first and hit first. Even crews in heavily armoured tanks could be rattled by incoming rounds striking the turret and hull, especially when they could not spot the enemy. Even an enemy force equipped with better tanks could be driven off by a hard, aggressive ambush. The tank crew's mantra of 'spot first – shoot first – hit first' is as true today as during World War II.

Tank skirmishes, as in most forms of combat, often went to whichever side achieved surprise, sometimes making for very one-sided actions. Anyone who has studied the war has likely read accounts of German tank crews, usually in a Tiger or Panther, inflicting enormous casualties on the enemy, knocking out dozens of Shermans, Cromwells or T-34s. While such instances did happen on occasion for both sides, on a smoky, dust-filled battlefield full of noise and shellfire, it can be hard to tell who hit what. Particularly suspect are the accounts of Waffen-SS veterans, many of whom wrote self-serving memoirs in the 1950s in an attempt to salvage their reputations.

Still, the Germans were often able to inflict heavy armour losses, largely because from mid-1943 on they were almost always on the defensive. Attackers nearly always suffer more losses than defenders. It is notable that when the Germans were fighting offensively, such as in the Ardennes in 1944, their loss ratios were markedly higher.

World War Two saw the development of the tank as a weapon at the tactical and operational levels to a high level. The massive numbers of tanks produced allowed large scale armoured operations at a scale not seen before or since. In the end, however, success still came down to the tank crewmen, struggling through exhaustion, cold, heat and the stress of combat to take the fight to the enemy.

BELOW: This Sherman, supporting infantry in Belgium in September 1944, has a "Culin device' on the front for pushing through hedgerows in Normandy, and extra armour plates over vulnerable points on its hull. (US NATIONAL ARCHIVES)

Early War Tanks 1939–42

Pre-war designs entering combat

ABOVE: The Crusader served as Britain's primary cruiser tank through 1942, though it saw combat only in North Africa. Crusaders were fast, but their thin armour and small 40mm gun (later replaced with a six-pounder) were disadvantages. (IWM TR157)

ABOVE: The German Pzkpfw. III was Germany's primary medium tank through 1942 and proved capable of moderate upgrades to keep it serviceable. This example from Panzer Battalion 40 advances near Vasonvaara, Finland in July 1941. (SA-KUVA)

ABOVE: The Soviet Union built small numbers of the large, multi-turreted T-35, armed with three cannon and up to seven machine guns. Most were lost due to mechanical breakdown. This T-35 of the Soviet 67th Tank Regiment is being examined by its German captors. (BUNDESARCHIV)

ABOVE: The Soviets developed the T-26 from a British Vickers design, over 10,000 were built. This one met its end at the hand of Finnish troops in 1940. (SA-KUVA)

ABOVE: The Soviet KV2 had a massive turret mounting a 152mm cannon. Its combat record was mostly unsuccessful. This example was captured and taken back to Germany for testing, then taken by the Americans in 1945. (US NATIONAL ARCHIVES)

ABOVE: Britain built 955 Mark IV (also known as the A13) cruiser tanks and they served in France and North Africa. These tanks of 1st Armoured Division are on exercise in the UK in April 1941. (IWM H9065)

RIGHT: A line of American-built M3 and M4 medium tanks at Fort Knox, Kentucky, ahead of a company of M3 light tanks. All three models saw their first combat with the British Army in North Africa. (US LIBRARY OF CONGRESS)

BELOW: The first Churchill tanks carried heavy armour, but the armament proved light. The tank saw many upgrades and variations. It was intended for infantry support. (IWM TR219)

ABOVE: German infantry crouch behind a Panzer I during an attack in Karelia, May 1942. Intended purely as a training tank, shortages meant the Panzer I saw extensive service in the first three years of the war. (SA-KUVA)

RIGHT: The M13/40 served as Italy's primary tank during the war. Its poor service record is due more to the lack of crew training and support than the tank's qualities, which were average for an early war tank. (US NATIONAL ARCHIVES)

RIGHT: The Renault R35 carried a short, low velocity 37mm cannon with a coaxial machine gun. Almost 1700 were built, making it the most numerous French tank in 1940. (US NATIONAL ARCHIVES)

ABOVE: Almost 2,700 Valentine tanks were supplied to the Soviet Union during the war, where it was prized for its reliability and armour protection. The British Army used it in North Africa. This propaganda photo was taken at the factory in Smethwick. (IWM P233)

ABOVE: This early model Panzer IV-D carries the short-barrelled 75mm gun, intended primarily for fire support. Less than 300 were available for the invasion of France in 1940 but by late 1943 it was one of Germany's primary tanks. (DUTCH MOD)

ABOVE: The Soviet T-34 surprised the Germans in 1941 with its capable 76mm gun and good armour protection. These two tanks are moving at night during the Soviet counterattack at Stalingrad in December 1942. (UKRAINIAN ARCHIVES)

ABOVE: The Tiger I appeared in late 1942 and was then the most formidable tank in the world. This photo shows a captured Tiger on display in the US for familiarisation, along with US soldiers wearing enemy uniforms. (US NATIONAL ARCHIVES)

BELOW: Two Shermans of the 9th Queen's Royal Lancers at El Alamein, November 1942. When the Sherman entered service, it ranked among the best tanks in the world. (IWM E18972)

Late War Tanks 1943–45

New designs and upgrades to the older ones

ABOVE LEFT: The Sherman soldiered on in Allied service throughout the war with various upgrades to keep it competitive. The M4A3E8, nicknamed the 'Easy 8,' had a 76mm cannon, wider tracks and an improved suspension for better cross-country performance. (US NATIONAL ARCHIVES)

ABOVE RIGHT: The Tiger II's firepower and armour protection made it a dangerous opponent, but poor reliability and Germany's fuel shortages meant few Allied tank crews ever actually fought one. (US NATIONAL ARCHIVES)

RIGHT: The M26 Pershing marked a leap forward in US tank design but came too late in the war for more than a few to see combat. This column of Pershings is heading toward the front, evidenced by the muzzle covers and turrets facing rear. (US NATIONAL ARCHIVES)

BELOW: The Churchill saw gradual improvements in armament as the war progressed and was also modified into several useful variants. The Churchill Crocodile flamethrower tank proved effective at assaulting enemy fortifications; it towed its fuel behind it in an armoured trailer. (IWM TR2313)

ABOVE LEFT: A Comet of the 2nd Fife and Forfar Yeomanry, 11th Armoured Division crosses the Weser River in April 1945. The Comet derived from the Cromwell but carried a powerful 17-pounder cannon. (IWM BU3200)

ABOVE RIGHT: The British Army modified about 2,100 Shermans with 17-pounder guns, nicknamed the Firefly. They were generally issued one per troop to spread anti-tank capability in each unit. (IWM B10358)

LEFT: By 1943 production of Panzer IVs incorporated the longer barrelled 75mm cannon, thicker armour and drivetrain improvements. This knocked out example has been hurriedly stripped; note the 75mm rounds on the ground, hull and turret. (US NATIONAL ARCHIVES)

LEFT: The M24 Chaffee began to replace the Stuart tank as the standard US light tank from December 1944. It offered no improvement in armour protection but carried a much more powerful 75mm cannon. (US NATIONAL ARCHIVES)

RIGHT: The Panther vies
with the T-34 in the
argument for the war's
best all-around tank.
Its blend of firepower,
armour protection
and mobility made it
superior in some respects
even to the heavier
Tigers. (BUNDESARCHIV BILD
183-H28356)

RIGHT: The British Army
built the Challenger using
the Cromwell chassis
mated to a large turret
with a 17-pounder gun.
It was often used in place
of the Firefly in units
equipped with Cromwells.
(IWM B11045)

BELOW LEFT: The Soviet
Union produced a series
of heavy tanks named
after Joseph Stalin.
These JS-2 tanks carried
a massive 122mm gun,
but its separate-loading
ammunition gave it
a slow rate of fire, a
disadvantage in tank
combat. (RUSSIAN ARCHIVES)

BELOW RIGHT: Nicknamed
the 'Jumbo,' the M4A3E2
Sherman assault tank
had additional armour
plate; its frontal armour
was up to 180mm thick.
Only 254 were built.
(US NATIONAL ARCHIVES)

ABOVE: The major improvement made to the T-34 was the T-34/85, with a new larger turret mounting an 85mm cannon. The bigger turret allowed space for a commander, gunner and loader, greatly improving the fighting qualities of the tank. US and Soviet generals are inspecting this tank crew a few days after the war ended. (US NATIONAL ARCHIVES)

ABOVE: British airborne forces used the US-designed M22 Locust during Operation Varsity. Landed by gliders, the small tank carried a 37mm gun and a .30-calibre machine gun. It did not perform well during the operation and was not used in action again during the war. (US NATIONAL ARCHIVES)

ABOVE: In North Africa, British workshops installed 75mm guns from wrecked Shermans into damaged Churchills, creating the Churchill NA75. Over 200 conversions were made and they were issued in the Italian theatre. (IWM NA23277)

RIGHT: Much has been made of the German Maus super-heavy tanks, but they never saw combat and were essentially a waste of resources. The surviving prototype is in the Kubinka Tank Museum in Moscow. (TANK MUSEUM)

Armoured Fighting Vehicles

Serving alongside the tanks

ABOVE LEFT: Tank destroyers generally possessed good firepower but thin armour. Designed to fight enemy tanks, operationally they saw more use as assault guns for the infantry. These US M10 76mm tank destroyers are firing at German outposts in Aachen, October 1944. (US ARMY)

ABOVE RIGHT: Britain's Universal Carrier served as a general-purpose light armoured vehicle. These soldiers of 8th Rifle Brigade are handing out chocolate to Dutch civilians in September 1944. The gun barrel at the bottom of the image suggests this is an anti-tank unit with six-pounder guns. (IWM)

RIGHT: Germany produced various types of Sturmgeschutz (assault guns, abbreviated StuG), often using older tank chassis. These StuG III Gs are in Finnish service, evidenced by the *hakaristi* symbol, similar to but not linked to the Nazi swastika. (SA-KUVA)

ABOVE: Germany also put captured material to use. This Marder III self-propelled anti-tank gun is built on an obsolete Czech tank chassis and mounts a captured Soviet 76.2mm cannon. This example was captured by the US Army after it was abandoned in North Africa in 1943. (US NATIONAL ARCHIVES)

ABOVE: Armoured cars saw wide use in most armies. These German vehicles are a Sd.kfz 234/2 with a 50mm anti-tank gun (near) and a Sd.kfz 234/3 with a 75mm howitzer. The Germans mainly used their armoured cars for reconnaissance but armed them to fight when needed. (POLISH ARCHIVES)

LEFT: The United States issued thousands of half-tracks to its own troops and distributed thousands more to its allies. They were used as personnel carriers and in a number of support roles. This halftrack of the US 10th Armored Division is moving past a burning village after engaging German snipers, 17 April 1945. (US ARMY)

BELOW LEFT: Self-propelled artillery, such as this US M7 Priest 105mm howitzer carriage, allowed artillery units to keep up with fast-moving tanks and motorised infantry. This vehicle of the 191st Tank Battalion is firing on enemy targets at the Anzio beachhead in March 1944. (US ARMY)

BELOW RIGHT: Germany produced over 15,000 Sd.Kfz 251 halftracks but still never had enough to fully equip the infantry forces in its panzer and mechanised divisions. This halftrack advances in Latvia in June-July 1941. (BUNDESARCHIV)

Anti-Tank Weapons

Mines to handheld weapons to towed cannon

ABOVE: This German tank-hunting team has both the reloadable Panzerschreck and single use Panzerfaust anti-tank weapons. They are taking cover behind a knocked-out US M4A3 tank in France, November 1944. (POLISH ARCHIVES)

ABOVE: The British Army issued the Projector, Infantry Anti-Tank (PIAT) beginning in Tunisia in 1943. It fired a hollow-charge bomb which could penetrate over 100mm or armour plate. (US ARMY)

ABOVE: Towed anti-tank guns saw wide use by infantry regiments and specialised anti-tank units. This is a US M1 57mm, a license-built version of the British 6-pounder with a longer barrel. (US ARMY)

TOP LEFT: Mines ranked among the top causes of lost and damaged tanks. They were often deadly to drivers and crew positioned in the hull. Crew in the turret had a better chance to survive. (US ARMY)

TOP RIGHT: A US soldier holds a German Panzerschreck next to an American M1 'bazooka.' The Germans developed their larger version from bazookas captured in Tunisia. It could penetrate up to 210mm of armour. (US ARMY)

ABOVE LEFT: Early in the war, armies issued anti-tank rifles as a defensive weapon. As tank armour improved, these became less effective. These Soviet troops are defending a position outside Moscow using a PTRD-41 14.5mm anti-tank rifle. (RUSSIAN ARCHIVES)

ABOVE RIGHT: More tanks were lost to anti-tank guns than enemy tanks. This German PaK 43 88mm gun is emplaced in a bandstand to overlook a crossroads in a Dutch town, November 1944. (IWM CL1519)

LEFT: Soldiers often improvise. These troops of the US 9th Infantry Division have rigged a twin bazooka launcher using a jeep's machine gun mount. (US ARMY)

Matilda II

British early-war workhorse

RIGHT: This Matilda II of the 6th Armoured Division shows the tank's solid appearance and turret armament. (IWM H9218)

In the first two years of the war the Matilda II was the UK's most fearsome and effective tank. Designed as an infantry tank, the Matilda II was a larger version of its machine gun-armed predecessor, the Matilda I. British military thought at the time infantry tanks were required to be well-armoured and moderately armed, but they did not need to be fast as they were intended to accompany troops at little more than their walking pace.

The Matilda II fit this description well, for better and (later in the war) worse. It carried three inches of frontal armour, proof against almost all anti-tank weapons in 1939-40. The only effective weapon against the Matilda was the German 88mm gun. Matilda's armament included a two-pounder (40mm) cannon, comparable to most tank guns at the time, and a coaxial Besa machine gun. The cannon had adequate performance against early-war Italian and German tanks, though it lacked a high-explosive round for use against anti-tank guns and enemy troops. Matildas were slow, only 24kph (15mph) on roads and 14kph (9mph) cross country.

The four-soldier crew included a driver in the hull and the commander, gunner and loader in the turret. In many tanks of the period the commander had to lead the tank and operate the armament, difficult to do in action. The presence of a gunner allowed the commander to focus on leading, a critical advantage in combat.

BELOW: A trio of Matilda IIs in North Africa near Tobruk in 1941. The nearest tank is named 'Go To It.' Note how the tank commanders are using their hatch lids a partial cover from frontal fire. (IWM T10128)

Matildas first saw major combat in France in 1940 at the Battle of Arras, performing well although the Allied attack ultimately did little more than delay the advancing Germans. In North Africa, the Matilda was valuable in the British counterattack against the Italian invasion in 1940. It performed well against German tanks in the desert until 88mm guns rendered the British tank vulnerable. Always short of tanks in the desert, the German Afrika Corps made use of captured Matildas when they had them. By 1942 the Matilda was withdrawn in North Africa but it continued to serve in Asia and the Pacific, where it remained effective until the end of the war.

Cromwell

Late war British cruiser tank

Combat experience in North Africa convinced the British military that the well-armoured but slow infantry tank had limited value on the evolving battlefield. They chose to develop a new cruiser tank with a reliable engine, decent armour and a more powerful main gun. The resulting design, the Cromwell, proved a good balance of all three.

It 75mm main gun was comparable in performance to the same calibre weapon on the Sherman and used the same ammunition, easing logistical burdens. Cromwell's powerful and reliable Rolls-Royce Meteor V-12 engine made it faster than the Sherman and it presented a lower profile, making it harder to spot and hit. The tank could reach speeds of 40mph but was often restricted to 32mph because the ride at the higher speed was very hard on the crew. While armour was thicker than the Sherman in places, it was not sloped, reducing its effectiveness.

Many British crews preferred it to the Sherman, but competing production demands meant Britain could not build enough Cromwells to completely equip its armoured divisions, so the two models served together, with the Sherman being the most numerous tank in British service. The tank's speed and low profile made it an effective reconnaissance vehicle. The British army equipped the reconnaissance units in its armoured divisions with Cromwells, effectively giving each division another tank battalion. This allowed these scouting units to fight to gain battlefield intelligence or defend against an enemy attack.

While the Cromwell suffered against German Tigers and Panthers in Normandy after the D-Day invasion, no Allied medium tank could perform better. Against other German armoured vehicles, it proved quite effective. Around 4,000 Cromwells rolled out of British factories before the war ended. They equipped Free Polish armoured regiments as well.

A close-support version of the tank carried a 95mm howitzer. Postwar, the Cromwell saw service in the Korean War until leaving service in the mid-1950s.

ABOVE: A Cromwell negotiates a small rise in Normandy. This tank has been fitted with an exhaust hood to redirect engine smoke downwards, making the tank harder to spot at a distance. (CANADIAN ARCHIVES)

LEFT: A Cromwell of the 7th Armoured Division leads a column of vehicles off of Gold Beach on 7 June 1944. The tank still has its wading equipment attached and a Sherman Firefly is behind it. (IWM B5251)

M4 Sherman

The Allies most widely used tank

ABOVE: An M4A3 Sherman of the US 12th Armored Division near Schneeberg, Germany in March 1945. This tank, named 'Was Ist Das,' carries the long-barrelled 76mm gun.
(US NATIONAL ARCHIVES)

RIGHT: A 75mm-armed Sherman in Italy. This model has the more rounded cast hull. The crew's stances hints at this being a posed shot for the cameraman. Note the large wine jug on the tank's right fender.
(US NATIONAL ARCHIVES)

The American upgrade was a high-velocity 76mm cannon; its anti-armour performance was better than the 75mm but less than the 17-pounder. It also fired a less effective high-explosive round than the 75mm; this was problematic in the field where tanks spent most of their time engaging anti-tank guns and fixed defences.

The Sherman's armour protection proved inadequate against German anti-tank weapons in 1943-45. These problems with its armament and protection have led it to be widely criticised, but the Sherman was reliable and easy to maintain. A Sherman which came ashore at Normandy could carry its crew to the German border with simple routine maintenance. No Tiger or Panther could have done that.

In that regard, the Sherman is perhaps best described as a general's tank. While an individual tank crew might well prefer the protection of the larger German tanks, senior leaders needed a vehicle that could be built in large numbers, transported overseas and kept in service by the thousands for months on end. The Sherman fit that bill better than any other tank in the war. Interestingly, the name 'Sherman" was given to the tank in British service; during the war, American soldiers seldom if ever used the name, instead simply calling it the M4. Postwar, however, the name took spread and took hold.

The Sherman is the ubiquitous American tank of the war, although nearly every Allied nation used them. Widely distributed under Lend-Lease, its combat debut came in British service in North Africa in 1942. At the time it was one of the best tanks in the world, and although it was extensively modified throughout the conflict, it could not keep pace with the continually improved anti-tank weapons fielded during the war.

Initially the Sherman carried a 75mm cannon which was effective against most of its opponents in 1942. This gun was ineffective against the mid-war generation of German tanks like the Tiger or Panther. The British Army mounted a much more effective 17-pounder gun with much greater armour penetration, but there were never enough of them available.

Tiger

Powerful and fearsome but a drain on resources

The Tiger tank is perhaps the most famous tank of World War Two. The Tiger series is well-regarded for its powerful armament, thick armour and reasonable mobility for a heavy tank. Less well considered were its poor mechanical reliability and high fuel consumption. Nazi Germany produced the tank in two iterations.

The Tiger I's initial development began in 1937 and it entered combat in September 1942 near Leningrad. It went on to serve across the Eastern and Western Fronts and North Africa. The Tiger carried up to 100mm of armour, making it difficult for enemy guns to pierce. Its 88mm KwK 36 cannon could penetrate up to 138mm of armour at 1,000 metres using Armour Piercing, Composite Rigid (APCR) ammunition. Until the Allies began to field their own heavy tanks in late 1944-45, the Tiger could destroy almost all Allied tanks at extended ranges. Several German 'tank aces' achieved their high kill ratios using the Tiger I. Germany produced 1,347 Tiger Is before production ended in August 1944.

The Tiger II, also called the King Tiger or Royal Tiger, was a larger version with thicker, sloped armour up to 185mm thick and a more powerful KwK 43 88mm gun. This weapon used a large cartridge casing with more propellant, allowing the Tiger II to penetrate up to 223mm of armour at 1,000 metres using APCR. 492 were built before the war ended.

Tigers proved fearsome opponents in combat, particularly when the Germans were fighting defensively, when the Tiger's slow speed and mechanical issues were less of a problem. The very name Tiger could invoke fear in Allied tank crews. However, Tigers were expensive. They used enough resources to build several other armoured vehicles such as Panzer IVs or assault guns. Their heavy weight strained their drivetrains; Germany lost more Tigers to mechanical breakdown and fuel shortages than enemy tanks.

Despites its deadly reputation, there were never enough Tigers to make a difference in the war's outcome. Today there are only two operable Tigers left in the world: a Tiger I at the UK tank museum in Bovington and a Tiger II at the French tank museum at Saumur.

LEFT: This trio of Tiger Is are on a sunken stretch of road in Western Ukraine. The slab-sided Tiger I provoked fear in its opponents. The cables draped over each tank's hull are for use in recovering stuck or broken-down tanks. (BUNDESARCHIV)

BELOW: Despite its power and size, most Tiger IIs ended their war like this example in April 1945, being pushed off the road by a bulldozer after breaking down or running out of fuel. (US NATIONAL ARCHIVES)

Panther

Germany's best medium tank

The Soviet T-34 tank gave the German military quite a shock in 1941, spurring them to build a counterpart. Some thought was given to simply copying the Soviet tank outright, but this idea was soon scrapped in preference to building an entirely German design. The new vehicle, soon named the Panzer V Panther, emulated the T-34 in its well-sloped armour and also had a powerful Maybach engine able to propel the tank at up to 55 kph (34 mph). The Panther's high velocity 75mm KwK 42 could penetrate 149mm of sloped armour at 1,000 metres.

Hitler had high hopes for the Panther and ordered 250 to be ready for combat for the impending summer offensive. However, the design remained immature and when it first saw action at Kursk in July 1943 many were lost due to overheating, and both fuel and oil leaks which could cause fires. These problems were resolved over time and the tank became much more reliable, though the design always had problems with the fuel pump and transmission. Although classified as a medium tank, the Panther weighed as much as some heavy tanks.

Those problems aside, the Panther performed effectively on the battlefield. At closer ranges, its 75mm gun outperformed the Tiger I's 88mm, though the 88 did retain its superior penetration at longer distances. It proved very effective against Allied tanks on both fronts in Europe. Most Allied tanks had difficulty penetrating the tank's sloped frontal armour, but its side armour was much thinner. Allied tank crews generally went for a flank shot on a Panther if possible.

Germany produced 3,964 Panther tanks through March 1945. Over 250 Panther turrets were installed as fixed defensive emplacements in Germany's various defensive lines. After the war the UK kept the factory open for a short time and had a small number of Panthers built for testing purposes. France and Romania both operated Panthers in their own armies for a few years after the war. Several dozen still exist today in museums and as monuments, including six believed to be in running condition. In 2015 a Panther tank was among the military relics found in a German pensioner's basement.

T-34

Soviet battle tank

The T-34 vies with the Panther in the argument over the war's best tank. While the Panther is usually hailed for its overall quality and capability, the T-34 earns its placed in the running due to its simplicity, durability and ease of construction. It was not the best at anything, but it was a good compromise of firepower, mobility and armour protection.

The Soviet Union fielded large numbers of light tanks in the 1930s, but needed a medium tank which could withstand anti-tank fire, carry powerful armament and reliably traverse the vast distances of the nation. The T-34 emerged from that development effort; to demonstrate its capability, engineer Mikhail Koshkin drove two prototypes 700km from Kharkov to Moscow and presented them to Stalin. The tank entered service in 1941.

Small numbers of T-34s were available when Nazi Germany invaded in June 1941. Along with the KV-1 heavy tank, the T-34 proved quite a shock to the Germans. Shot from their 37mm anti-tank guns bounced off its thick, sloped armour. Only 88mm cannon and heavy artillery pieces stood a chance of stopping it, while the T-34's main gun could penetrate any German tank at normal combat ranges. In 1941, most T-34s were lost to shortages of ammunition, fuel and lack of trained crew. Its appearance forced the Germans to conduct crash efforts to field larger tank and anti-tank guns and create improved panzers such as the Panther.

The T-34 went through a series of upgrades during the war. The initial production version carried a 76.2mm cannon and had up to 45mm of armour. These upgrades included better armament, thicker armour and improvements to the drivetrain. The final model, the T-34/85, had up to 90mm of armour and an 85mm cannon. It is believed almost 84,000 T-34s and variants were produced, including some built after the war.

The Soviets retained the T-34 in service after the war and distributed it widely as military aid. They saw service in numerous postwar conflicts and running examples are common in museums and even private collections. Until 2022 a T-34/85 sat on a corner in Bermondsey, London, frequently repainted by local artists.

ABOVE: A T-34/85 with tank riders sitting near the Brandenburg Gate in Berlin in May 1945. Note the wire sections attached to the tank as a standoff against shaped-charge weapons such as the panzerfaust. (USAMHI)

LEFT: A Soviet tank company commander briefs his tank commanders before an attack in 1943. Note the models he is using to demonstrate the company's scheme of manoeuvre. (TANK MUSEUM)

Captured Tanks

All armies put captured enemy weapons to use and tanks were no exception. In the chaos of combat, tanks which broke town, ran out of fuel or took damage were often abandoned, particularly when a force had to retreat. Often such captured armour was taken out of the combat area for study, but these tanks also saw improvised use against their former owners.

Most use of captured armour consisted of individual tanks employed by units in the field. These tanks would be used until they were out of ammunition, suffered irreparable mechanical failure, or were destroyed. Captured armoured vehicles had to be clearly marked to minimise the risk of destruction by friendly troops. It also required leaders to inform frontline troops of their presence.

In a few instances, armies formed units out of captured tanks.

ABOVE: This US-built M3 Stuart light tank went to the Soviet Union as part of Lend-Lease, was eventually captured and put to use by the Germans. It is seen here knocked out in Estonia in 1944. (ESTONIAN HISTORY MUSEUM)

RIGHT: The Germans referred to a captured tanks as a 'buetepanzer,' or 'loot tank.' German troops captured this M4A3 Sherman at Aschaffenburg in March 1945. It was knocked out by the M36 tank destroyer on the left. Note the hastily applied crosses to identify it to other Germans. (US NATIONAL ARCHIVES)

ABOVE: This Panzer IV is being moved to the rear after being captured intact by Allied forces near Grandvillars, France in October 1944. The turret is turned to the rear to show the vehicle is not a threat to friendly troops who might see it. (US NATIONAL ARCHIVES)

ABOVE: Tanks might be captured more than once. The Germans seized this Polish 7TP in 1939 and put it to use in France, where it was 'liberated' by the US Army in 1944. Germany often used obsolete tanks in anti-partisan duties. (US NATIONAL ARCHIVES)

Commonwealth forces in North Africa captured enough Italian tanks early in the war to equip at least one Australian unit, While the Germans put captured Matildas to use. On the Eastern Front, the Germans captured enough T-34s and even some production facilities to field formations up to company size. Over time the Soviets captured enough German tanks to likewise group them into distinct units.

ABOVE: The 4th Battalion, Coldstream Guards captured this Panther Ausf G in a barn in Overloon in Autumn 1944. The Guardsmen prized the tank for its long-range accuracy and used it in several operations until its fuel pump failed in February 1945. (IWM)

LEFT: Germany produced more Sturmgeschutz III assault guns than any other armoured vehicle. American troops captured this example, which has ad hoc concrete armour added to its front. (US NATIONAL ARCHIVES)

LEFT: New Zealand troops recapture a Matilda tank the Germans have been using in North Africa, 1941. Note the German flag and markings. (AUSTRALIAN WAR MEMORIAL)

Cadet Orlik in Poland, 1939

A young Polish tank commander mauls two panzer forces

The German invasion of Poland in September 1939 is often summed up as a rapid German victory, but it was a much more difficult fight than is commonly portrayed. German casualties and equipment losses were much higher than the Nazi regime admitted at the time. While Poland ultimately lost, German troops at times ran into very effective Polish resistance. One such example comes from a young Polish officer cadet who ably led a platoon of obsolete tankettes against two superior Panzer forces.

Edmund Roman Orlik, 21 years old when Germany invaded, began his military career at an air force school but soon transferred to the Polish Armoured Warfare Training Centre. After completing the two-year course, he went to university in Warsaw to study architecture. As war loomed, the Polish Army conscripted Orlik as a reserve officer cadet in the 71st Armoured Squadron. This unit had one company of armoured cars and another of tankettes.

The unit's leaders placed Orlik in command of a 'demi-platoon,' consisting of three TK and TKS tankettes, small, tracked vehicles with a crew of two, a driver and a gunner/commander. Compared to the latest German panzers, the TK series was tiny, poorly armed and lightly armoured. Tankettes were considered obsolete by many armies even at the beginning of the war, but they were on hand and had to be used. The two models were alike in most respects, but the TK carried a 7.92mm machine gun while the TKS was armed with an automatic 20mm cannon which could penetrate 25mm of armour plate at 300 metres range.

Orlik commanded a cannon armed TKS driven by Corporal Bronislaw Zakrzewski. The other two Tankettes reportedly carried only machine guns, as cannon-armed models were in short supply. The 71st reported to the Wielkopolska Cavalry Brigade, part of the Poznan Army, stationed in Northwestern Poland near the German border.

German armoured and infantry forces poured across the border on 1 September 1939 and within a few days the Poznan Army was in danger of being cut off by a pincer movement. However, on 9 September the Wielkopolska surprised several columns of the German 24th and

30th Infantry Divisions, inflicting 1,500 casualties and taking 3,000 prisoners. The 71st participated in the action against the 30th Division. On 14 September the 71st engaged German tanks, Panzer IIs of the Panzer Regiment 36. The Poles knocked out three Panzer IIs, though it is uncertain which Polish tankette crews struck the blows.

On 18 September, Orlik's three tankettes began a scouting mission along the forested road to the village of Pociecha. Near an intersection, Orlik was inspecting enemy tank tracks along the road when the Poles heard the sound of approaching tanks. In his account, Orlik moved his TKS into an ambush position off the road and ordered his machine gun armed vehicles to fall back into the woods a short distance since they would be ineffective against tanks.

Soon a trio of German tanks appeared – one Panzer IV armed with a short-barrelled 75mm gun and two Czech-built Panzer 35(T)s with 37mm cannon, all far superior to his lone tankette. A German nobleman, Lt. Victor von Ratibor, commanded the Panzer IV. Orlik waited until he had a shot at his opponent's thinner side armour and opened fire.

The first burst struck the lead German vehicle, a Panzer 35(T). It stopped as smoke poured from its ▶

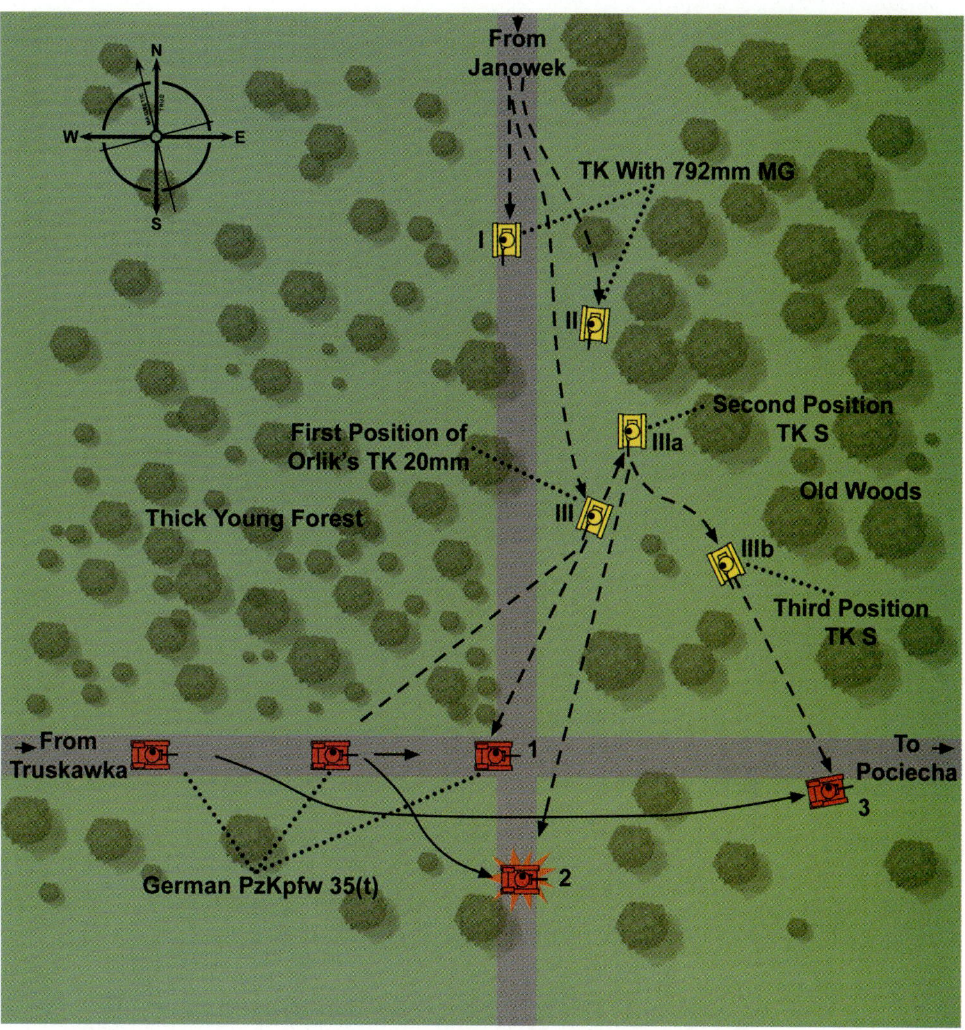

LEFT: The TK series of tankettes were practically obsolete when the war began but were used to good effect by brave Polish crewmen. This machine gun armed variant could be effective against infantry. (POLISH ARCHIVES)

hull and the crew bailed out. The other two tanks left the road and fired wildly, unable to locate their attacker. The Panzer IV moved behind the smoking Panzer 35(T) but moments later appeared as it moved past the wreck. Orlik fired a burst which appeared to have no effect. However, a second burst tore into the German tank's side armour and started a fire, possibly from detonated ammunition. No one got out of that tank.

Orlik turned his attention to the third tank as his driver switched positions. The Polish officer cadet spotted the last German tank moving through some bushed alongside the road, only 60 metres away. Another burst knocked that tank out as well. The Poles took several of the German tank crewmen prisoner and pulled some wounded and dead crewmen from the destroyed tanks. Lt. von Ratibor was badly burned and died within minutes but was later identified by the hunting license he carried. The Polish ambush succeeded in destroying three German tanks.

Later that day, Polish forces drove the Germans from Sierakow, northwest of Warsaw. Anticipating a counterattack, Orlik's and two

other cannon armed tankettes were deployed to a defensive position along with some 37mm antitank guns and an artillery battery with 75mm guns. The next morning at 10AM, the counterattack began.

More Panzer 35(T)s of Panzer Regiment 11 and Panzer Battalion 65 crossed an open plain southeast of the town. Polish Captain Zbigniew Szacherski recalled, "On a plain in front of us, only 800 metres away, there were swarms of German tanks… this was the first battle in our sector fought not by men against men, but rather shellfire against steel." He counted 30 to 50 German tanks approaching.

The lead German tank took a hit from an anti-tank gun, starting the action. Several other panzers rolled to halt, stopped by the artillery, but the rest came on, spreading out. Orlik positioned his tankette among some shallow sand and gravel pits, providing his tiny vehicle cover. His 20mm gun was loaded with captured German ammunition. Spotting two enemy tanks a few hundred meters away, he had the driver pull out of their pit and opened fire, seeing the flash of an impact on the panzer's side armour. That tank stopped shooting

but the other kept firing. Orlik put another burst into it, knocking it out as well.

Corp. Zakrzewski nudged Orlik; it was time to get back to cover. A third Panzer spotted them, however, and charged, firing it 37mm cannon. Orlik returned fire, but his rounds landed short, ricocheting into the air over the Panzer. The German's next round slammed into the ground right in front of the tankette. Orlik adjusted his aim and fired another burst, but there was no effect. Just as he began to fear the next German shot, the Panzer ground to a halt, its hatch opened and the crew emerged, hands raised in surrender.

Orlik had them sit atop his tankette as they returned to cover. After dropping off his prisoners, Orlik returned to the battle, knocking out a fourth tank just before a trio of panzers targeted him. Firing several more bursts, he managed to knock out two of them, but the third kept coming. Orlik took careful aim and pulled his trigger – on an empty weapon! All of his ammunition expended, the driver manoeuvred wildly as the German tank fired at them, rounds flying all around the tankette. Finally, they found some cover out of the enemy's

BELOW: The Polish military restored this TKS tankette, armed with a Hotchkiss machine gun, and uses it in historical displays. Note the gunner's periscope above the armament and the two French-pattern helmets strapped to the hull above the spade. (POLISH MOD)

view. When Orlik climbed from his tankette and chanced to leave cover to locate their attacker, the panzer sat immobilised, abandoned by its crew, the victim of another Polish gun.

The battle ended soon after. The Poles claimed to have knocked out 20 Panzers, while German records listed 38 tanks lost, though it is uncertain how many were recovered and repaired. Orlik's tally was seven enemy tanks damaged or destroyed. Other Polish accounts dispute this number or attribute them to other tank crews, which is common in the chaos of battle, where multiple crews might fire at one target with no way to know who struck the telling blow. Still, if Orlik knocked out only half the claimed number of tanks, he might well be the war's first 'tank ace.'

The surviving tankette crews drove their vehicles to Warsaw, including Orlik. They fought on until the city surrendered on 28 September. Orlik evaded capture and some accounts say he joined the resistance. He survived the war to become an architect, dying in an accident in 1982.

Despite fearful odds, Orlik and his fellow tankette crewmen proved able to cause heavy losses among superior German panzer forces on at least two occasions, proving the tanker's adage of 'see first, fire first, hit first.' Using ambush tactics and strong defensive positions with cover and concealment, they made the German army pay dearly for its conquest.

BELOW: A line of Panzer 38(T)s crossing a field. The Nazi flag on the tank's engine deck is for identification to friendly aircraft. (BUNDESARCHIV)

Panzer versus Char at Stonne

When the German Wehrmacht advanced through the Ardennes region during the invasion of France in May 1940, it hoped to seize the French city of Sedan. Located on the east bank of the Meuse River, Sedan could serve as a launching point for a drive to the sea to trap the Allied armies in Belgium. Such a split would doom the Anglo-French forces to defeat.

Using fast-moving panzer and motorised forces, Germany captured Sedan and crossed the Meuse, overcoming the French defences. However, the elevated Mont Dieu plateau sits south of Sedan, and German General Heinz Guderian, then commanding the XIX Armee Korps, worried the French could launch a counterattack from the plateau against the Sedan bridgehead. He ordered 10th Panzer Division to hold the plateau while other armoured forces began the race west toward the coast.

Atop the plateau sits the village of Stonne, about 15 km (nine miles) from Sedan. It had a commanding view of the area. The Germans needed it to shield the bridgehead while the

French required it as a jumping-off point for their counterattack. This set the stage for a violent and difficult battle. German accounts often refer to the Battle of Stonne as the 'Verdun of 1940.' One German officer later paid grim tribute to the battle by

saying, "There are three battles I can never forget: Stonne, Stalingrad and Monte Cassino."

The French gathered forces for their attack, slowed by bomb-damaged towns and roads choked by fleeing civilians. Many of their tanks suffered breakdowns en route and the units lacked sufficient refuelling equipment, requiring an extended period simply to refuel their vehicles. A small French reconnaissance group including a pair of Panhard 78 armoured cars reached Stonne on 14 May 1940. These troops ran into French infantry fleeing from an earlier French counterattack at Sedan, who warned them of German panzers in the area. Shortly after, a French infantry battalion arrived with two 25mm and one 47mm antitank guns.

The Germans advanced toward Stonne with the motorised *Grossdeutschland* Regiment in the lead, attached to 10th Panzer Division as a reinforcement. Before dawn on 15 May, a battalion of that regiment neared Stonne with a tank force of six Panzer IVs and 5 light Panzer IIs. These tanks had to move up a sharp hairpin turn in the road leading into

The lead Panzer IV bore the number 700, a command tank for a German captain. The French fired and the first 25mm round tore through the tank's armour. The 25mm round was solid shot, containing no explosive charge, so the gunner fired several more rounds into the tank to ensure its destruction.

Next, they took aim at the second Panzer IV, number 711. The first shot hit the driver's visor, decapitating him. This shocked the radioman next to the dead man into inaction. The rest of the crew bailed out while the French gunners poured more fire into the tank. When the crew returned to the tank later, they found the radioman had been shot trying to get out.

Now the French set their sites on the third Panzer IV, its line of fire blocked by the tanks in front of it. It too was hit, starting a fire which spread to the tank's ammunition. The tank blew apart in an enormous explosion. The French gun crew hitched their weapon to its tractor and moved to a new position as German infantry entered the town. Several Panzer IIs moved around ❯

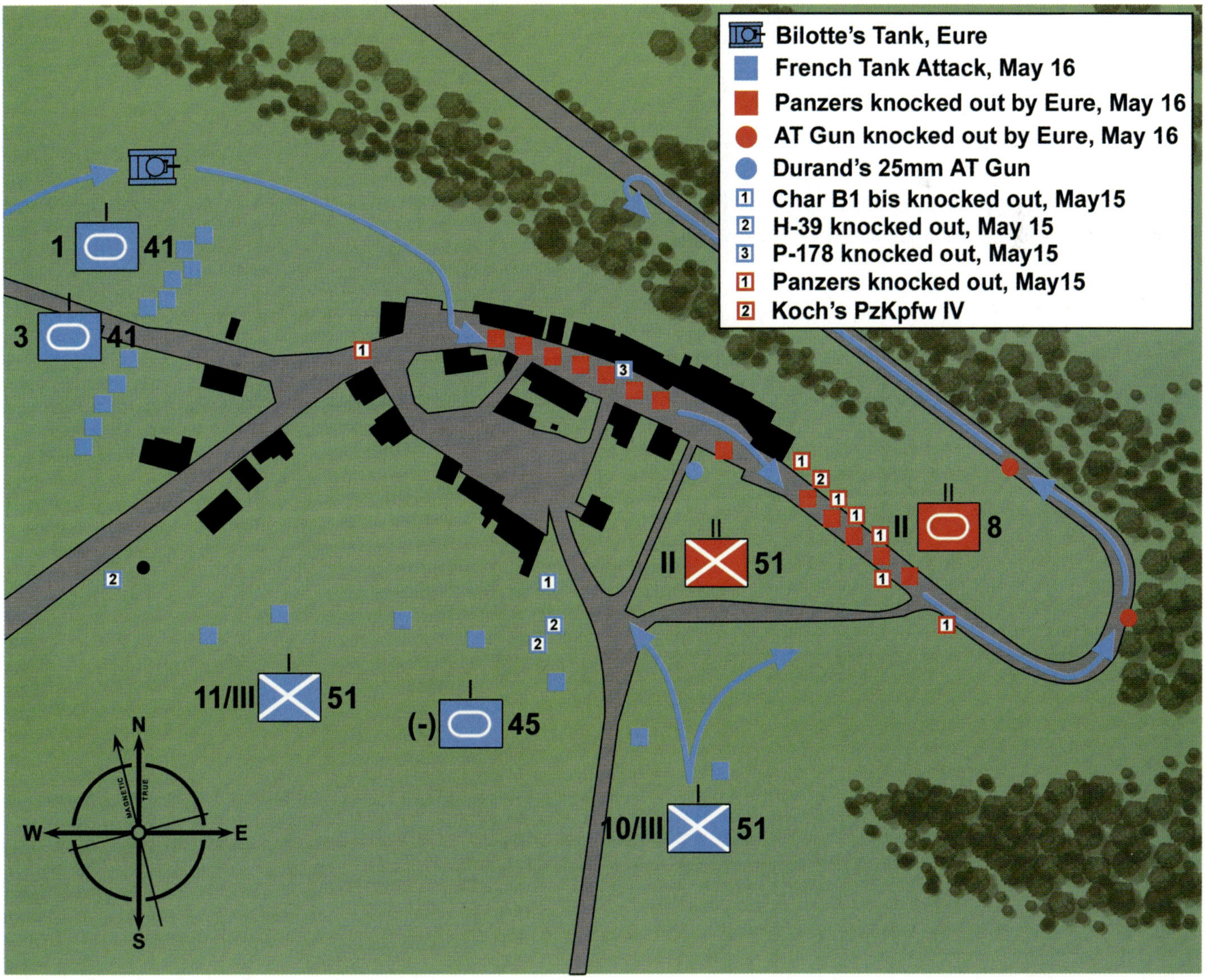

LEFT: Panzer IV number 711 sits abandoned after the battle. Despite being immobilised, the crew used it to knock out several French tanks during the battle. They scrounged ammunition from other knocked out tanks to stay in action. (US NATIONAL ARCHIVES)

Stonne. An artillery barrage struck the town just before the panzers moved into it. After the barrage lifted the tanks moved along the road toward the main street of Stonne.

The French anti-tank gunners stood ready for them. The nearest 25mm gun had the three leading Panzer IVs in its sights. Commanded by a cool-headed veteran sergeant, the crew waited until the first tank was only about 40 metres away. At such close range the 25mm could penetrate up to 47mm of armour; the early-war Panzer IV had only 30mm of frontal armour at most.

ABOVE: A Panzer II crosses a pontoon bridge near Sedan the day before the battle for Stonne began. The light Panzer II carried a 20mm cannon and was markedly inferior to most other tanks during the fighting in France. (US NATIONAL ARCHIVES)

RIGHT: A German soldier inspect a knocked-out Panzer IV. The small calibre penetration of the turret was likely from a Hotchkiss 25mm gun. (BUNDESARCHIV)

RIGHT: The Panzer IV was intended primarily as a support tank, armed with a low-velocity 75mm cannon. It still had to engage enemy tanks in combat. (BUNDESARCHIV)

the disabled Panzer IVs to support those troops.

The fighting became close and intense; three Panzer IIs fell to the 25mm guns and both French armoured cars were knocked out. One Panzer II advanced completely through the town only to be hit by the other 25mm gun. Despite the heavy tank losses, the action went in favour of the Germans and the French infantry withdrew. The remaining Panzer IVs took up defensive positions in the town.

The French quickly organised a counterattack using what tanks were available. The first wave contained 13 Hotchkiss H-39 light tanks, armed with a 37mm cannon. As they approached the town, the German crew of Panzer 711, immobilised earlier, returned to their tank and opened fire, knocking out two French tanks at 600m. The rest continued, taking fire from German 37mm anti-tank guns but managing to destroy two more panzers. Although they managed to reach Stonne, without infantry support they were soon forced back.

The next French attack involved three enormous Char B1 bis tanks, heavily armed and armoured. The Germans had not encountered them before, and the infantry quickly withdrew. The French tanks set up on the town's southwest side, unable to advance further without infantry support. Nevertheless, when the French spotted German anti-tank guns being set up, they advanced, firing their machine guns. The Germans opened fire with their 37mm cannon, only to watch in dismay as their rounds simply bounced off.

Two of the antitank guns were soon destroyed but the third, commanded by an observant German sergeant, noticed a grill on the Char's left side and fired at it. The round went through and set the tank afire. Another Char came within range of Panzer 711. Its gunner, Sergeant Karl Koch, later recalled, "It was a real monster and we had no idea the French had tanks like that. We fired 20 shots at it without success. However, after a few more shots, we managed to knock off its track." The third Char appeared and Koch fired at it without effect until a few hits jammed its turret and knocked off another track. It eventually exploded. Afterward the crew of 711 left the tank as it was out of ammunition.

The next French attack came with a punishing artillery barrage and was well coordinated. It included three more Char B1 bis and a handful of lighter French tanks supporting a reinforced battalion of infantry. The Char B1 bis tanks stopped to provide covering fire with their hull-mounted 75mm guns, while the light tanks advanced with the infantry. This succeeded in pushing the Germans out of Stonne.

The French infantry dug in while the tanks withdrew to replenish their fuel and ammunition. The Germans responded with an air attack by Stukas and an artillery barrage which drove the French infantry out of the town. However, by mid-afternoon they re-occupied it before the Germans could. The French heavy tanks went with them.

LEFT: The Hotchkiss 25mm anti-tank gun proved effective early in the war. Here, captured French troops evacuate a casualty under German guard, passing the now-abandoned gun. (FRENCH ARCHIVES)

The German postponed a planned counterattack until early evening, their troops exhausted. That attack pushed the French out of the north end of Stonne, but they stubbornly held on to the south end throughout the night. The French planned a new attack for the early morning of 16 May. A total of 14 heavy Chars were available, along with some H-39s to support the infantry.

The attack began before dawn with a 45-minute artillery bombardment. The French heavy tanks moved in immediately after the barrage lifted and attacked German tanks and anti-tank guns. Two of the French tanks broke down and a third flipped over into a gully, but one of them had great success.

The Char B1 bis commanded by Captain Pierre Billotte swung around the French left flank and managed to enter the town on the west side, reaching the main street. There, a column of German tanks sat in a tightly packed line, preparing for a counterattack. Most of them were Panzer IIs, with a few Panzer IIIs and IVs for support. Billotte ordered his driver to use the use the hull-mounted 75mm cannon to engage the front panzer while he used the 47mm gun in the turret to attack the last one in the column. With the front and rear tanks immobilised, the rest of the German tanks could not move.

Billotte calmly directed his tank down the street, destroying every panzer in the trapped column. Continuing along the main street, Billotte spotted an approaching column of German tanks and knocked these out as well. German return fire failed to penetrate the French tank's 60mm thick armour; Billotte's tank took 140 hits but remained in action. Rounding the hairpin curve, he destroyed another pair of 37mm anti-tank guns before turning back. Billotte claimed 13 panzers during the battle.

German and French forces fought over the town for the rest of the day; during one action a Char B1 charged into a German position and ran over some of the infantry. Afterward the fighting continued for another week, but without the use of tanks. Both sided suffered heavy casualties in soldiers and armour, the German losing 25 tanks and the French 33. Today a Char B1 bis sits in Stonne at a memorial to those who fought there.

BELOW: The Hotchkiss H-39 provided close support to infantry during the Battle of Stonne and worked in concert with the heavy Char B1 bis. (US NATIONAL ARCHIVES)

The Battle of Arras

The defeat that saved the British Army

After the German army seized the French city of Sedan and crossed the Meuse River, it sent the fast-moving Panzer divisions west toward the channel coast to cut off the Allied armies. This included the British Expeditionary Force (BEF) along with French and Belgian troops. The panzer force moved quickly enough it proved difficult for Allied commanders to react; most of them were not ready for the pace of modern warfare.

This fast pace created opportunities, however. The panzer forces soon became spread out, leaving gaps in their lines. The rest of the German army still travelled by foot and horse, as armies had for centuries. It sometimes took days for them to catch up. One of those gaps appeared near the French city of Arras. If the Allies could gather enough tanks and troops quickly, they could cut the German axis of advance and perhaps blunt their offensive long enough to consolidate and counterattack.

The initial plan was to launch attacks on Arras from north and south, but the French armoured forces to the south were dispersed among the infantry units and needed time to concentrate. The BEF's armoured forces, the 1st Army Tank Brigade, north of Arras, were kept together and could move to Arras immediately. The chief difficulty was in moving their armour some 130 miles (209km) on roads choked with refugees and subject to German air attacks.

Once in place, the British organised their forces into two groups, simply called the Left and Right Columns. Each contained a battalion of the Durham Light Infantry (DLI), along with anti-tank, artillery and reconnaissance units. The Right Column had 7 Royal Tank Regiment (RTR) while the Left Column had 4 RTR. Between the two columns the British tank force included 58 Matilda Is, 16 Matilda IIs and 14 Mark VIB light tanks. As the Matilda II was their most capable tank, planners divided them equally between the two armoured regiments.

The plan called for the columns to move in parallel, descending from Vimy Ridge (of World War One fame) and moving south, passing Arras to the west. Then, they would pivot east and move south of the town and establish a new line, oriented east. Their right flank would be covered by a French mechanised division, 3DLM, which had two tank battalions equipped with Somua S-35 and Hotchkiss H-39 tanks.

The German *XV Panzer Korps* sat in the path of the British columns. The 7th Panzer Division had the mission of isolating Arras from the

west. Commanded by *Generalmajor* Erwin Rommel, this division had 36 Panzer IV and 106 Panzer 38(T) tanks. At this stage of the war Rommel was a rising star and was still building the reputation he would establish in North Africa the following year. The 5th Panzer Division sat on Rommel's right flank, assigned to support him; it was delayed, however, and never took part in the battle. On Rommel's left flank was the inexperienced SS-Totenkopf Division.

The British attack got off to a bad start. Commanders lacked sufficient time to brief their subordinates. The infantry was still arriving at their assembly areas, so the tank units were unable to coordinate with them. The tank brigade had moved under radio silence; arriving near Arras, they discovered most of the radios had drifted off frequency and there was no time to retune them. Only the light tanks had working radios since they used them for scouting missions. The rest of the crews had to use hand signals and flags.

Both sides planned to begin their advance at 2PM on May 21, 1940. The Germans got moving first. Rommel accompanied his tanks but soon had

to go shepherd his motorised infantry units, which had fallen behind. Thirty minutes later the British Right Column got moving, but 7RTR took the wrong road and drifted west.

They had a brief firefight with what turned out to be a French unit before reorienting and advancing toward the village of Duisans.

After seizing the village, the 7RTR commander, Lt. Col. H. Heyland, realised he was behind schedule and decided to bypass the next objective of Warlus and move to the town of Dainville. This decision inadvertently helped the Germans, as Panzer Regiment 25 was also advancing near Warlus and would have fared poorly against 7RTR's Matilda IIs.

The Left Column ran into Infantry Regiment 6, one of Rommel's lost units and attacked into its flank. The German infantry had 37mm antitank guns, but their fire bounced off the thickly armoured Matildas. British cannon and machine gun fire drove the Germans back, many of their anti-tank guns crushed under the tracks of British tanks.

Sgt. H.D. Reed commanded a Matilda I. "I distinctly remember Squadron Sergeant Major Armit, just ahead of me, getting repeated hits on his tank turret. Everyone was firing away briskly," he said. "I claimed a motorcycle and sidecar outfit, which divided itself around a tree… I could not get at an ant-tank gun concealed in front of a railway bridge but decided to polish off two lorries parked nearby. Next thing, a flash and a cloud of smoke – even inside the tank I felt the blast. This had been an ammunition lorry and its demise also put paid to the gun."

As the Left Column routed the German 6th Regt. and continued their advance, 7RTR attacked Infantry Regiment 7. Rommel, now aware

❯

LEFT: 7th Panzer Division primarily used the Panzer IV and Panzer 38(T) tanks, seen here during the invasion of France. Shortages of Panzer IIIs compelled the Germans to use the Czech-built 38(T) in large numbers. (BUNDESARCHIV)

LEFT: These Matilda IIs, the nearest named 'Glanton,' bogged down in mud at Arras and were abandoned. Glanton was later set on fire for a propaganda photo. (BUNDESARCHIV)

BELOW: The small Matilda I had good armour but carried only a Vickers .50 or .303 machine gun. This example is guarding the approaches to Dunkirk as British troops file past. (IWM)

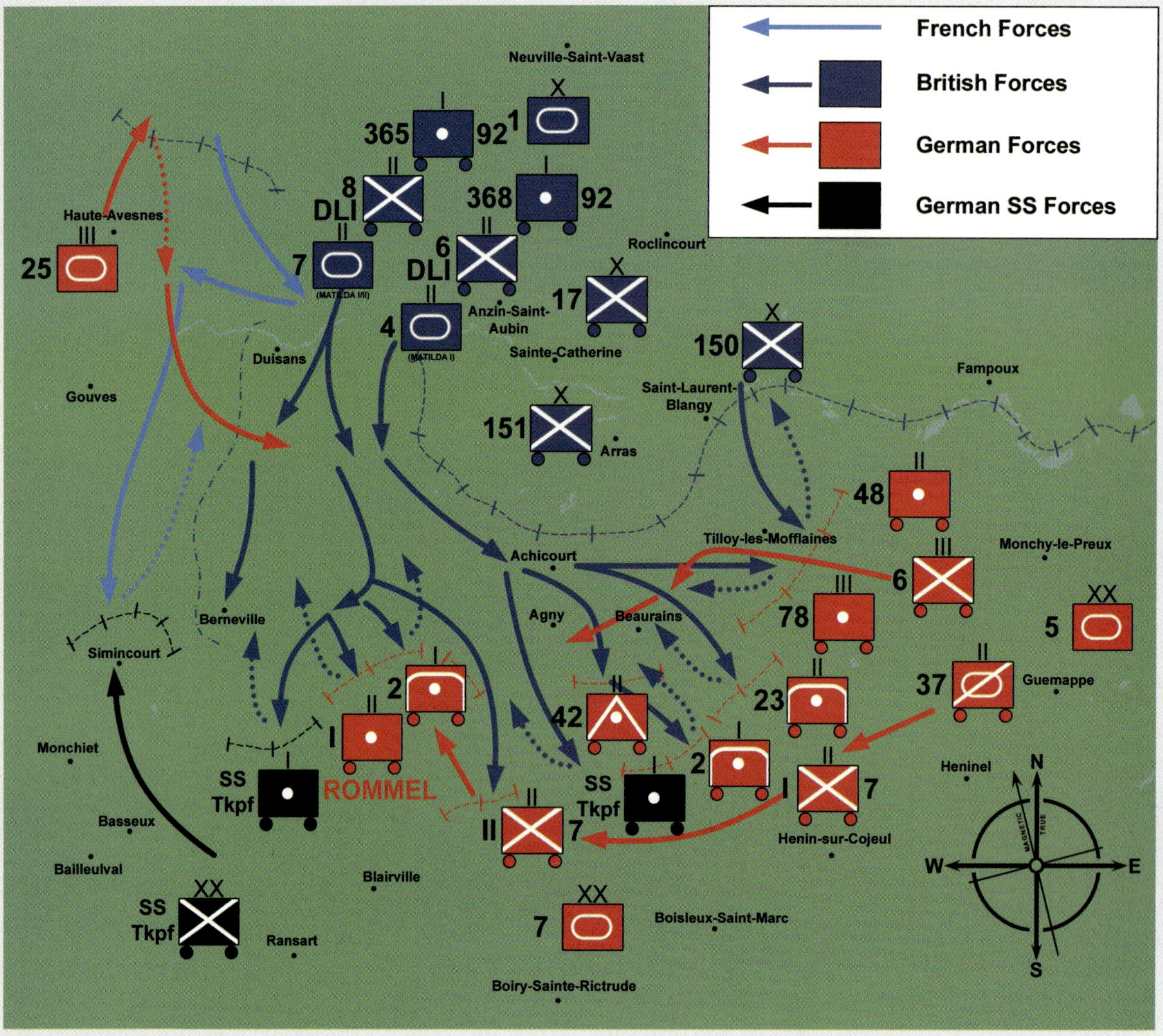

of the danger, personally brought forward a battery of 88mm guns and his heavy artillery. The '88' was an antiaircraft gun but had been designed with a secondary anti-tank role. The tide started to turn against the British as the 88 could penetrate even the Matilda's armour. An air attack by Stukas caused further damage as British tanks began to burn. The 4RTR commander, Lt. Col. Fitzmaurice, died when a German shell punched through the armour of his Mark VIB tank.

4RTR soon lost 20 tanks and received the order to withdraw. As they pulled back, a few tanks from Panzer Regiment 25 arrived and joined the fighting. However, their hasty, ill-coordinated attack failed and all the panzers were lost. 4RTR formed a defensive line and prepared its nine remaining tanks for a German counterattack.

7RTR succeeded in routing Infantry Regiment 7, which fled into the lines of the SS-Totenkopf. Several of the SS units panicked and ran as well.

BELOW: Rommel studying maps with a group of his officers during the Invasion of France. Note the Panzer 38(T) tanks in the background; they were the primary tank issued to 7th Panzer Division. (BUNDESARCHIV)

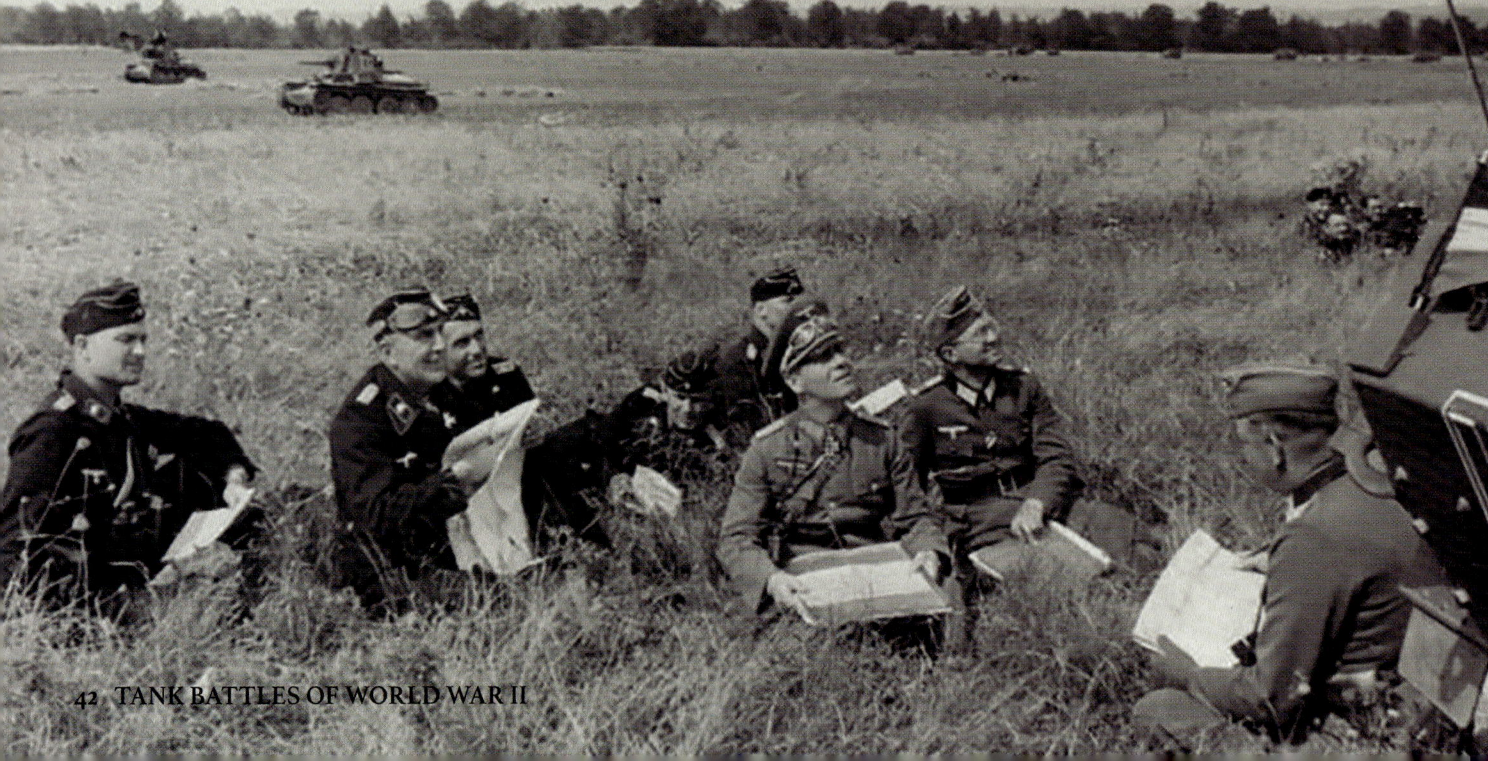

The British column continued forward but soon ran into Rommel's gun line and lost several tanks and Lt. Col. Heyland, who was killed. Major John King took command and punched through the gun line with several Matilda IIs. Rommel remained with the gun line most of the day, so focused on the battle he did not notice when his orderly was killed right next to him.

King led his Matildas in a duel with the German guns. They overran a battery of anti-tank guns and ran into four panzers. They knocked out all four, setting two afire. King's tank led the way when an artillery round struck it, jamming the turret and wounding the gunner. Spotting another anti-tank battery, the British overran it as well, crushing the guns under their tracks. King spotted an 88 and put his tank in some dead ground it couldn't fire into. He carefully manoeuvred into a spot where he placed machine gun fire on the German gun, suppressing the crew until he got close enough to destroy it. Soon, King's tank and another Matilda were knocked out and had to be abandoned. Both tanks sat just in front of the German's last line of defence.

The Right Column got no further that day. The infantry returned to the recently captured villages and prepared a defence. It took time for the Germans to ready their counterattack; Rommel, so focused on commanding the gun line against the British attack, lost focus on what the rest of his division was doing. The main body of Panzer Regiment 25 reached it objectives but never received further orders, so it stopped.

It didn't receive new orders to attack into the British rear until 7PM.

That attack met defeat. The German tanks ran into a line of two-pounder guns from 260 Anti-tank Battery. While the British gunners tore into the panzers, French tanks from 3DLM tore into the German flank. At least 12 panzers were lost along with a few French tanks and British guns. Rommel also sent in an infantry attack on the British lines, well-supported by artillery. Just as the British troops ran low on ammunition, six French tanks blasted their way through the German force. The British infantry rallied around these tanks and the whole group fought their way back to Vimy after midnight, ending the Battle of Arras.

The British counterattack at Arras failed in its objective but inflicted heavy casualties on the Germans. These losses worried the Wehrmacht High Command, who ordered a slowdown in the advance to the coast so its flanks could be strengthened, particularly at Arras. This gave time for the Allies to prepare for their evacuation at Dunkirk, one of the German coastal objectives. Combined with Hitler's decision to halt his tanks outside Dunkirk and let the Luftwaffe attack the port, Arras enabled 336,000 British, French and Belgian troops to survive, preserving the British Army to fight another day.

ABOVE: A German 37mm PaK 36 anti-tank gun in a defensive position. This weapon proved of mixed effectiveness against allied tanks during the battle of France. (BUNDESARCHIV)

LEFT: Two Panzer IVs advance through a French village. Note the open hatch for ventilation and the fuel cans stacked atop the turret. Short operating ranges plagued most tanks of this period. (BUNDESARCHIV)

Beda Fomm

British tenacity in the Libyan desert

ABOVE: The British anti-tank guns at Beda Fomm were 37mm Bofors mounted on lorries, known as a 'portee.' The Bofors was slightly less powerful than the British two-pounder, but still effective against Italian tanks. (IWM E2300)

RIGHT: The A9 cruiser tank carried a two-pounder cannon and two machine guns in small turret on the hull. In practice the extra machine guns overtaxed the crew and were usually left unmanned. (IWM E100)

The Italian army invaded Egypt in strength on 13 September 1940, advanced 100km, stopped and set up camp. Despite outnumbering British forces in Egypt, they awaited reinforcements, particularly tanks and artillery. While this invasion appeared lacking in aggressiveness, the Italians were short on motor transport, unlike their opponents.

The British Western Desert Force (WDF) began a campaign of harassment and patrolling to pin the Italians in place while organising a counterattack. This plan, Operation Compass, sought to push the Italians out of Egypt, but planners kept in mind the possibility of going further. The leader of Middle East Command, Gen. Archibald Wavell, wrote "I do not entertain extravagant hopes of this operation, but I do wish to make certain that if a big opportunity occurs we are prepared morally, mentally and administratively to use it to the fullest."

This British foresight paid off when their counterattack commenced on 9 December. The Italian's fortified

camps fell quickly to mechanised British task forces and the Italians were soon retreating toward the border. With the Italians back in Libya in disarray, the WDF commander, Lt. Gen. Richard O'Connor, realised his command of 36,000 could keep going, despite still being outnumbered by over three to one.

This led to a slow, fighting withdrawal for the Italians through eastern Libya, compelled by their lack of transport to use the coastal towns and road. By early February 1941 most of these towns lay in British hands, including vital ports such as Tobruk. The remaining Italian forces began a headlong retreat to link up with

the Italian divisions in central and western Libya.

This presented both opportunity and dilemma. British 7th Armoured Division could send a small force cross-country through the desert and intercept the retreating Italians farther down the coast at Beda Fomm. This would trap the Italians between the interception force and the Australians pursuing them down the coast. However, the WDF neared exhaustion after two months of combat. Its tanks and vehicles badly needed an overhaul and the available lorries could barely carry enough supplies to get there, much less keep a force in the field. If the Italians pressed hard enough, the entire force could be lost.

Maj. Gen. Michael O'Creagh, commanding 7th Armoured, decided the risk was worth taking. He dispatched Lt. Col. John Combe of the 11th Hussars at the head of a mixed force of armoured cars, infantry, anti-tank guns and artillery known as 'Combeforce.' The tanks would follow after a short stop for needed maintenance. On the morning of 5 February, 2,000 British troops and 140 vehicles set off across the desert. They reached the coastal road 16km south of Beda Fomm around noon.

The area contained open terrain with a few ridges running generally parallel to the road. British troops nicknamed a small hill near the road 'the Pimple;' it was one of the few spots allowing observation and would see heavy fighting. The only landmarks were a mosque and two windmills. Combeforce quickly established a roadblock and occupied the ridges. The infantry dug in and laid a few anti-tank mines, while the anti-tank guns set up on the ridges. The armoured cars formed screens to the north and south.

These preparations were still underway when the Italians arrived ➤

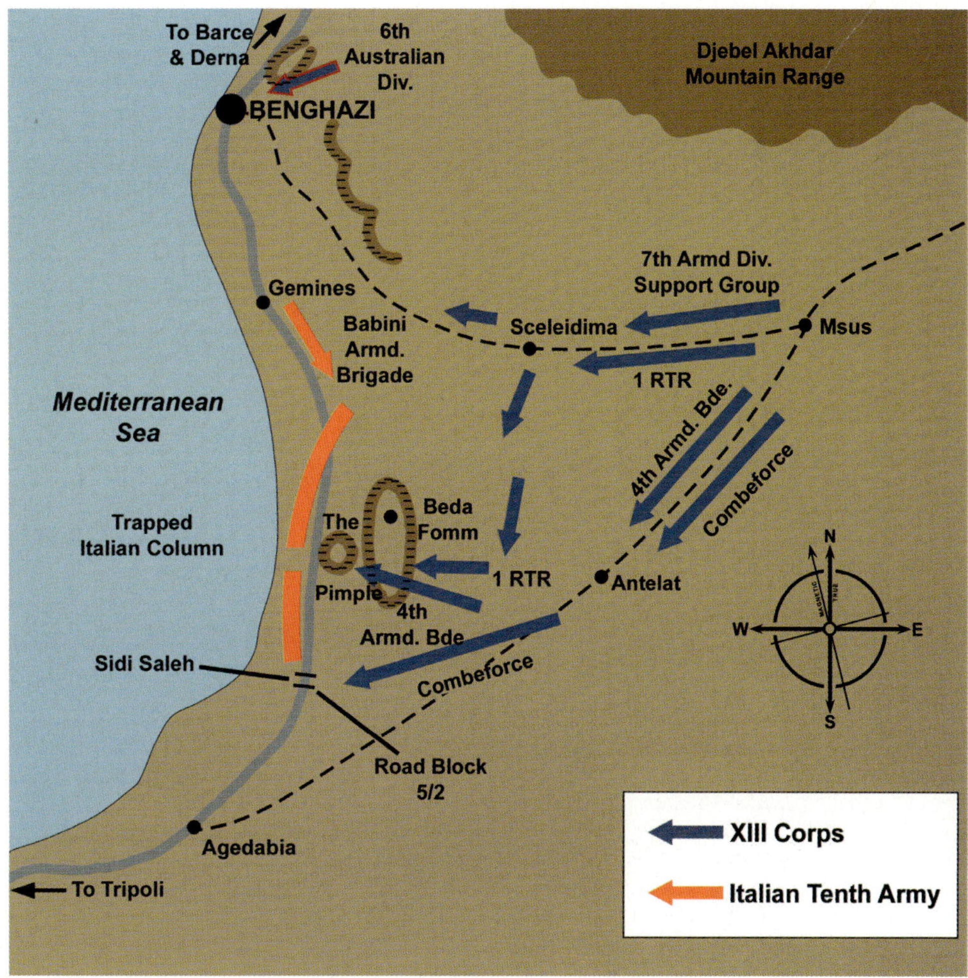

at 2:30 PM. Fortunately for the British this first enemy column were mostly rear-echelon troops. Combeforce's 25-pounder field guns pounded the Italians while the armoured cars harassed them with machine gun fire. Three Italian attacks failed but pressure was building as the tanks of 4th Armoured Brigade arrived in late afternoon.

Containing a mix of cruiser and light tanks, the brigade immediately went into the attack, one unit reaching Beda Fomm at 5:00 PM. The tanks shot up two columns of vehicles and artillery, using the light from a burning Italian fuel lorry to continue the fight after dark. One British sergeant of the 7th Hussars took a large number of prisoners but was armed only with a Very pistol (a flare gun). Fortunately, one of his prisoners, who had lived in the USA and spoke good English, gave him an automatic.

2RTR shot up a column of Italian transports. At the end of the column sat two Italian M13 tanks. Lt. Norman Plough parked his cruiser tank to cover them and sent Trooper Eldred Hughes to coax the crews out. Hughes knocked on the hatches with the butt of his revolver and took them prisoner. While marching them back, Hughes spotted an Italian officer in a dress uniform and took him prisoner as well. The trooper later received a Distinguished Conduct Medal (DCM).

Large numbers of Italians surrendered, but many fought on as more of them arrived, including more tanks and artillery. The British, running low on ammunition, siphoned the fuel from their lorries to keep the tanks and armoured cars mobile. The 25-pounders had only 30 rounds apiece. Tank strength stood at 22 cruiser and 45 light tanks, while the Italians had perhaps 200, though they were spread throughout the retreating columns now approaching the British defences.

The morning of 6 February proved windy and rainy with poor visibility. 2RTR, positioned on the Pimple, came under attack at 08:30 AM, with ten M13 tanks leading the assault. A group of A13 cruiser tanks from A Squadron, 2RTR, knocked them out from hull-down positions before moving a mile east, where they destroyed another seven tanks. C Squadron, using A9 and A10 cruisers, destroyed another eight M13s and took 350 prisoners.

By noon another 15 Italian tanks lay knocked out, but 50 more remained in action. Italian artillery pummelled the Pimple as the fighting continued. Trooper 'Topper' Brown of 2RTR later wrote: "...we never stopped firing at wagonloads of infantry or tanks... We definitely had a score of 20 M13s at the end of the day. At times we were getting overwhelmed...Italian artillery knocked out 4 RTR cruisers who ran out of ammo."

At 1:00PM some lorries arrived and resupplied the tanks with fuel and ammo, but Italian artillery had occupied the Pimple and it took several hours to dislodge them and retake the position. A few hours later 2RTR again had to pull back to rearm and refuel, leaving the Pimple to the Italians once more.

Meanwhile, about 30 Italian tanks and vehicles broke past 2RTR and attacked the roadblock at 9:00 PM. An anti-tank gun knocked out four tanks before a shell killed or wounded the crew. Four more tanks and some lorries got through the roadblock, but the remaining Italian attackers retreated. British defenders, reinforced by some newly arrived anti-tank guns, repulsed two more attacks in the dark, the last around midnight.

The Italians had about 30 tanks left and decided to make one last attack on 7 February at 06:30 AM.

LEFT: A British tank crew pauses for a meal in December 1940. Their tank appears to be a Mk. VIB, armed with two Vickers machine guns, one a .50 calibre and the other in .303. (IWM E1501)

the road past his position. He received an immediate DCM." Burton later manned a gun himself and helped knock out five more M13s. Artillery and infantry with anti-tank rifles destroyed the last Italian tank when it was just a few metres from the officer's mess tent. Afterward, Italian troops began surrendering in groups.

The British captured another 25,000 troops and enough serviceable enemy tanks to equip a regiment. This brought the total for Operation Compass to 110,000 prisoners and 380 tanks. O'Connor's daring achieved a great victory for the United Kingdom during an otherwise difficult period, earning him the nickname 'the little terrier, because he never lets go.' The real credit went to a few thousand tired, grimy British troops manning worn-out tanks and guns. Their tenacity and determination at Beda Fomm stopped an Italian force many times their size.

A heavy artillery barrage landed ahead of this desperate attempt, which managed to avoid the British armour and go in against the roadblock with its infantry and anti-tank guns. The M13s fired on the move as British anti-tank guns fired back. The British infantry managed to keep their Italian counterparts at bay for a while but were soon overrun, prompting them to call in artillery on their own positions.

The anti-tank gun crews stayed in the fight despite the artillery and enemy infantry. Major R.S. Burton of 106 Battery, Royal Horse Artillery, reported "All our anti-tank guns did very well... Sgt. Gould knocked out six tanks at extremely close range... getting some tanks as they ran down

LEFT: A column of Mk. VI tanks crossing the desert. The march route to Beda Fomm was strewn with rocks; rough going even for tanks. (IWM E443)

BELOW: An A9 cruiser kicks up dust as it advances. Movement in the desert produces clouds of dust making it almost impossible to move without being spotted at a distance. (IWM E101)

Easter Victory at Tobruk

The Afrika Korps' first defeat

RIGHT: A Panzer II knocked out at Tobruk. The fire was likely set well after the battle to make a more dramatic photograph. (AUSTRALIAN WAR MUSEUM)\

The war in North Africa was a back-and-forth affair. Italy invaded Egypt in September 1940, only to be thrown back by a British counterattack, Operation Compass, beginning in early December. The British Western Desert Force steadily pushed the unprepared Italian army, westward into Libya, capturing Tobruk on 22 January, and then decisively defeated the Italians at Beda Fomm and set up defences while Tobruk, with a good harbour, was fortified and improved.

Unfortunately for the British, circumstances compelled the withdrawal of much of their strength to reinforce Greece, soon under attack by the Germans. This drastically weakened the defences in the Western Desert. Simultaneously, German General Erwin Rommel arrived in Libya on 12 February with 5th Light Division, an armoured unit with 150 tanks. He quicky organised an offensive using his division and several Italian ones, including the Ariete armoured division. They advanced on 24 March and quickly pierced the weakened British lines.

Within three weeks Rommel pushed his forces 700km from Mersa Brega to Tobruk and was eager to push into Egypt. He had to take Tobruk, however. The Axis supply lines were too long to maintain momentum; seizing Tobruk gave them a good port to bring supplies forward by

sea. Also, Rommel could not leave the Tobruk garrison in his rear, as it was large enough to launch attacks into his supply lines. He wanted to take it quickly so he could resume his eastward offensive.

The garrison contained the 9th Australian division with three infantry brigades, with another brigade from the Australian 7th Division. Thousands of British troops manned machine gun units, anti-tank guns, artillery and a mix of armoured units with about 60 tanks. The Australian infantry also manned a large number of captured anti-tank and artillery cannon on an ad hoc basis, nicknamed 'bush artillery.'

Overall command fell to Australian Maj. Gen. John Lavarack.

Tobruk's defence lines stretched over 48km, including a small anti-tank ditch in front of barbed wire fences and minefields. Outposts placed every 700-1000m were manned by Australian infantry with machine guns and sometimes an anti-tank gun. Artillery supported the outposts and the tanks were formed into a mobile reserve to deal with armoured penetrations of the perimeter. Lavarack and his officers knew they could not prevent a concentrated panzer attack from getting through the perimeter, so the Australian infantry were instructed to let the

BELOW: A Panzer III passes a burning lorry in the desert in April 1941. In open desert with no landmarks, navigation was difficult. Compasses and accurate maps were essential; poor maps contributed to the German defeat at Tobruk. (BUNDESARCHIV BILD 1011-783-0150-28)

LEFT: Australian troops inspect a Panzer III knocked out during the battle. This tank was stopped near the anti-tank ditch and a post for barbed wire can be seen behind it. (AWM)

too." There were no anti-tank guns in this section of the perimeter, so Balfe's soldiers "fired on them with antitank rifles… they didn't attempt to come through, but blazed away at us and then sheared off east…"

As the Germans moved east, they suppressed the Australian outposts with gunfire. Meanwhile, 11 cruiser tanks of 1st Royal Tank Regiment (1RTR) moved toward the Axis force. When the Axis tanks neared the El Adem road, Australian troops manning Italian 47mm anti-tank guns opened fire, knocking out one Italian tank and damaging several others. Small arms fire disabled an Italian tankette and its crew was captured.

The Axis force detected a minefield and turned away from it just as 1RTR arrived. Both forces opened fire at long range. A British lieutenant reported knocking out two Panzer IVs, one Panzer III and an Italian tank for the loss of two A-10 cruiser tanks. Some British gunners reported watching their two-pounder shot bounce of the German tanks at 800m range. After this skirmish the Axis group withdrew southwards. That night German engineers tried to breach the ditch and wire in the dark, but aggressive Australian patrols drove them back.

Saturday, 12 April, passed without another attack. A German reconnaissance force supported by tanks drew artillery fire and British air attacks as soon as it appeared. The Germans suffered from poor maps, making it difficult to coordinate and navigate. They also needed time to regroup and prepare for a concerted attack. German leadership thought Tobruk was poorly defended and its troops were evacuating. ◗

tanks pass and use their machine guns and small arms to hold up the Axis infantry. This would separate them from the panzers, who would be dealt with using mines, artillery and tanks.

The first German attack took place on Friday, 11 April. Axis armour supported by infantry approached the perimeter along the road leading south from Tobruk to El Adem. They began probing the defences as the Australians in the nearest outposts called in artillery. They reported five German tanks destroyed by artillery

fire about 1,000m from the perimeter. Undaunted, the Germans advanced to 400m from the perimeter, where the Australians opened fire with small arms, slowing the German infantry.

Captain Balfe, an Australian infantry officer in the forward outposts, recalled, "About 70 tanks came right up to the anti-tank ditch and opened fire on our forward outposts… three waves of twenty and one of ten. Some of them were big German Mark IVs mounting a 75mm gun. Others were Italian M13s and there were a lot of Italian light tanks

BELOW: A 5th Light Division assembly area just before the first attack on April 11. The vehicles are spread out to reduce the chance of damage by artillery fire. (BUNDESARCHIV)

called for two battalions of panzers to punch through the defences and lead the Ariete division all the way to Tobruk. The panzers appeared about two hours later, moving slowly in the darkness.

Crossing the ditch after 05:00 AM, 38 Panzers with three self-propelled anti-tank guns advanced past the Australian outposts. Some of the panzers towed anti-tank and anti-aircraft guns or had infantry riding on their engine decks. The infantry jumped off the tanks and followed on foot once through the perimeter. The Australians made no attempt to stop the panzers but called in artillery on the infantry, inflicting heavy casualties and forcing them to stop. The panzers moved on without them.

The delays in the German assault allowed British and Australian artillery and anti-tank guns to set up on both sides of their line of advance. This included eight 25-pounder field guns and numerous two-pounder anti-tank guns. British tanks deployed toward the German right flank. The

ABOVE: A 25-pounder gun in action in the desert. At Tobruk these guns had good results against German Panzer IIIs and IVs. (IWM E14114)

RIGHT: Rommel with German and Italian officers surveying the Tobruk defences. His desire to take Tobruk quickly led to a rushed and poorly planned operation that ended in failure. (US NATIONAL ARCHIVES)

BELOW: 1RTR used cruiser tanks at Tobruk in April 1941, such as these A10 models, armed with a two-pounder cannon. (IWM E1001)

They were surprised to find a determined defence.

The main Axis attack occurred on Easter Sunday, 13 April 1941. The main effort came from the 5th Light Division, which formed up along the El Adem road. The Ariete Division sat on their left. Farther west, near the road to Derna, the Italian Brescia division made a demonstration attack to distract the Australians.

Due to the poor maps and lack of reconnaissance, the actual breaching point sat about four km west of the El Adem road. The Australian infantry watched the Germans forming up about four km from the perimeter. German infantry advanced with a few tanks in support, set up machine guns and started firing at the outposts. The Panzers seemed to be searching for a gap in the anti-tank ditch to cross. Darkness fell with infantry actions and artillery fire from both sides. Finally, around 02:30 AM, the German infantry managed to open a gap for the tanks. The plan

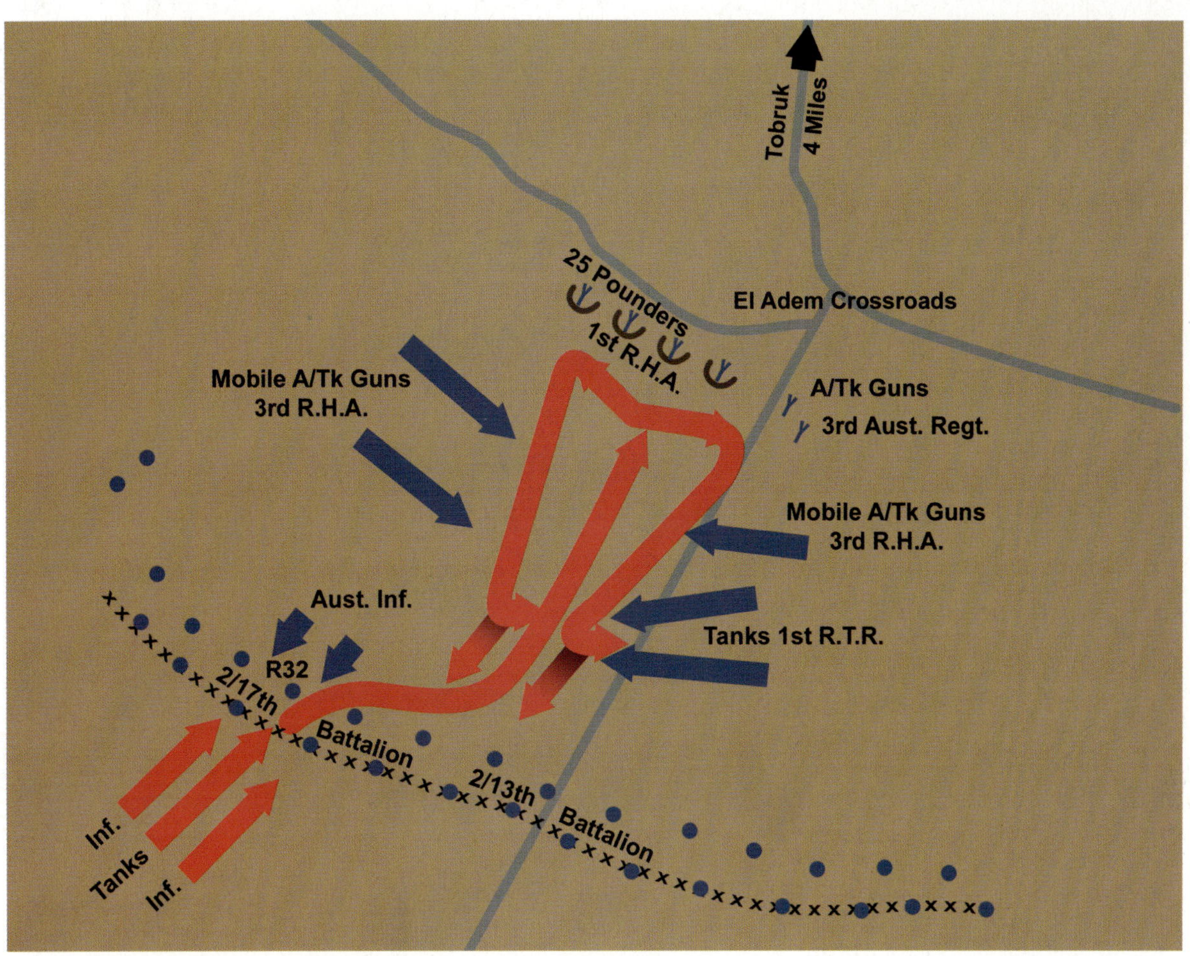

panzers attacked aggressively but they had entered a maelstrom.

The panzers advanced by bounding, one group moving up while another covered them. The British 25-pounders opened fire at 600m, the crews using open sights to engage the Germans. The artillery lacked armour-piercing rounds, but the heavy high-explosive shells quickly set five panzers ablaze and one Panzer IV's turret was completely blown off. Two panzers tried to flank the artillery but were knocked out by anti-tank guns. The leading German battalion decided to withdraw but ran into the second battalion behind them, causing confusion.

Two squadrons of cruiser tanks from 1RTR entered the battle next. As they approached the Germans, a British anti-tank battery, their two-pounders mounted on trucks, began hit and run attacks on the scattered German tanks. The Germans managed to knock out a 25-pounder and several anti-tank guns, but the battle was going against them.

German Lt. Joachim Schorm recalled the battle. "We are right in the middle of it with no prospect of getting out. From both flanks, armour-piercing shells whiz by at 1,000 meters per second... from every side, the superior forces of the enemy shoot at us." Finally, an order to withdraw came over the radio. Schorm and the other panzer commanders went back the way they had come, stopping to let wounded infantry climb aboard. Dust from explosions and smoke from burning panzers made it hard to see. Schorm wrote, "We have to press on to the south, as it is the only way through. Good God! Supposing we don't find it?"

Despite the fear of the moment, the Germans withdrew in good order. But their attempt to take Tobruk ended in defeat. A determined and active defence stopped Rommel's blitzkrieg in its literal tracks, costing them 17 more panzers. A second Axis attack on 30 April also failed. The defenders, soon known as the 'Rats of Tobruk,' held out until relieved in December 1941. Rommel finally captured Tobruk in June 1942, but the Axis forces abandoned it without a fight during the retreat after their defeat at El Alamein.

BELOW: A Panzer IV crossing a filled-in portion of the anti-tank ditch. Note the tank has a missing road wheel.
(AUSTRALIAN WAR MUSEUM)

Battle of Dubno June 1941

The largest tank battle in history

When Nazi Germany invaded the Soviet Union on 22 June 1941 in Operation Barbarossa, it sent over three thousand tanks across the border. The Soviets possessed 20-25,000 tanks, depending on source. This set the stage for large tank actions, most of which are relatively unknown today, lost in the chaos of the offensive, the narrative of German success and later, better known battles. One such action occurred around Dubno in Ukraine from 23-30 June. Also known as the Battle of Brody and by a few other names, it involved over 4,200 tanks between both sides.

Generalised narratives on Barbarossa tend to gloss over the first few weeks of the war, stating simply that the Germans achieved large victories and pushed the Soviets back all along the front. While this is true it is also an oversimplification. In places the Soviets put up stiff resistance and inflicted heavy casualties on the Axis forces, each small success weakening German prospects for total victory. Dubno is one such example.

Panzer Group 1, commanded by Generaloberst Paul von Kleist, spearheaded the offensive of the German Army Group South. It advanced toward Kiev in Ukraine, employing five panzer divisions (the 9th, 11th, 13th, 14th and 16th) in three corps, with 700-750 tanks. Their axis of advance sought to pierce Soviet lines at the junction of its 5th and 6th Armies. The Panzer Group benefitted from effective air support during the battle and had its own artillery and engineer units.

The six Soviet Mechanised Corps at Dubno (4th, 8th, 9th, 15th, 19th and 22nd) fell under the command of Colonel General Mikhail Kirponos. After managing to survive Stalin's purges of the 1930s, Kirponos distinguished himself during the 1940 Winter War with Finland. Unlike many Soviet officers who feared acting without specific orders, he was willing to act on his own initiative. This enabled his command, the

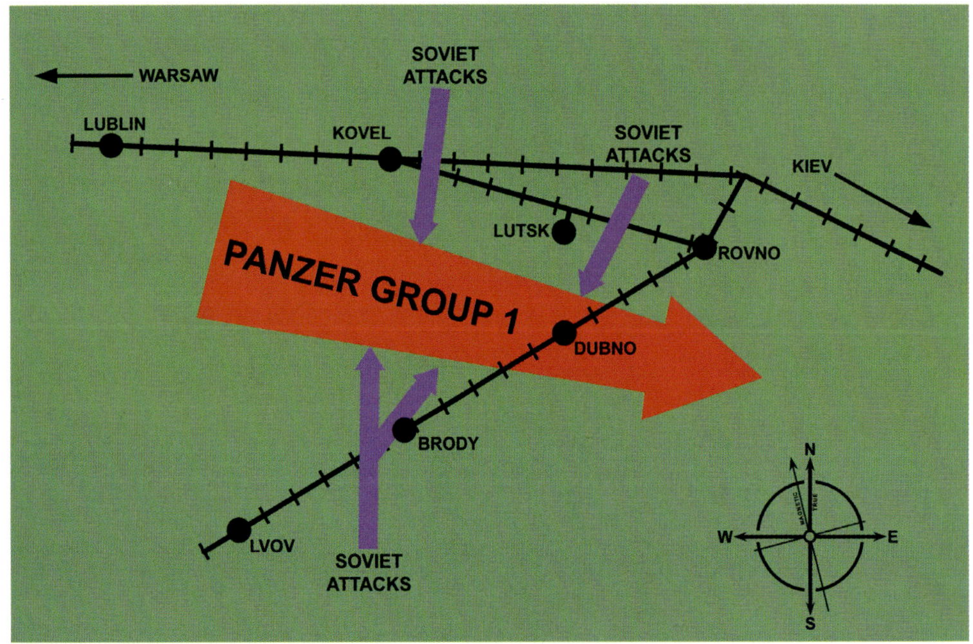

Southwestern Military District, to be somewhat better prepared and less surprised by the German invasion. His six corps controlled around 3,500 tanks, with perhaps 400-500 of them the new T-34 medium and KV heavy tanks. Light tanks such as the BT-7 and T-26 made up the remaining numbers.

Several Soviet weaknesses offset their numerical advantages. Abysmally low standards of training plagued their tank crews, who often abandoned broken-down tanks because they had no idea how to maintain them. Shortages of spare parts further increased tank losses. Insufficient numbers of trucks prevented units from moving infantry with the tanks or transporting supplies. Poor coordination hampered available air support. Communications often depended on civilian telephone and telegraph systems, subject to destruction and interception.

Despite these problems action had to be taken, and Kirponos devised a plan to conduct attacks along both flanks of Panzer Group 1. The Soviet 9th, 19th and 22nd Corps fell under 5th Army, north of the German force. The 4th, 8th and 15th Corps, belonging to 6th Army, south of the Germans. The counterattack began badly for the Soviets as their corps moved into position using the poor roads, hampering their ability to coordinate. Above, German aircraft bombed and strafed them. Some Soviet tank units blundered into swamps or marshes and became stuck.

All this meant the Soviet tanks met Panzer Group 1 in uncoordinated attacks, a few tanks at a time, rather than in an effective mass. A later German report noted: "Tank attacks generally were not conducted at a fast enough pace; frequently they were not adapted to the nature of the terrain." The poorly trained Russian drivers often exposed their tanks to enemy fire because they feared driving in low areas. This allowed the Germans to "bring the Russian tanks under fire at long range and to inflict losses before the battle had even begun. Slow and uncertain driving and numerous firing halts made the Russian tanks good targets."

Since most Russian tanks lacked radios, tank units tended to cluster around the command tank, waiting for hand signals or flags. This allowed the Germans to quickly identify command tanks and destroy them. Soviet troops tended to withdraw or surrender if they lost their leaders, as initiative was stifled in the Soviet army at the time.

ABOVE: Two Panzer IVs in Russia. The short-barrelled 75mm gun on these models was intended mainly or infantry support rather than anti-tank use. More panzers are in the background (BUNDESARCHIV)

BELOW: A burning T-34 near Dubno in June 1941. Only the German 88mm gun had a good chance of piercing its armour. (BUNDESARCHIV)

ABOVE: German soldiers inspect a knocked-out KV-2 tank. It carried a massive 152mm gun, but some of the KV-2s used at Dubno did not have ammunition. (POLISH ARCHIVES)

Not everything went the German's way. While German weapons made quick work of Soviet light tanks, T-34s and KV-1 and -2s proved much harder to stop. One German unit, equipped with a 37mm anti-tank gun, recorded "When the distance gets to 600m the gun opens fire. Almost every shot hits the target. The tracers from the shells are clearly visible. Then, however, we couldn't believe our eyes: our anti-tank shells were just bouncing off the tanks. The enemy tanks kept advancing toward us... firing at us with all their weapons."

On 26 June the battle began to reach its climax. The Soviet 8th and 15th Corps attacked north while the 9th and 19th Corps advanced south, planning to meet near Dubno and cut Panzer Group 1 in two. Fighting went on for days, with the Soviets taking horrible losses and the Germans resisting but taking casualties and tank losses of their own.

During the evening of 29 June 16th Panzer Division came under attack from both flanks, unable to continue any forward movement. The leading panzer companies ran into well-entrenched anti-tank guns and heavy fire from Soviet tanks. The fighting went on for hours; German platoons had to rotate tanks to the rear to replenish their ammunition and fuel. Near a highway, a mass of drunken Soviet infantry emerged from marshlands on both sides of the road, attacking the German division while Soviet tanks appeared on the road itself.

This attack soon threatened the division's artillery, support and anti-aircraft units. A withdrawal order went out and the German columns began a disordered retreat. It seemed the Soviets might succeed, but a few Germans stood their ground and poured fire into the advancing Soviets. Here, a tank crew methodically picked and engaged targets; there, a gun crew refused to limber their gun and retreat, instead staying in action. Together, they managed to stop the Soviet assault.

After dark, the Soviet tanks withdrew; a portion of 1st Battalion, 2nd Panzer Regiment, led by Major Hyazinth von Strachwitz, followed them undetected back to their lines. When it became light, the Panzer IIIs opened fire, causing chaos among the Soviet units and destroying several batteries of guns. This and other actions later earned him a Knight's Cross. Reinforcements rushed to 6th Panzer Division put an end to Russian chances to cut German lines.

Despite heavy losses (16th Panzer alone claimed 293 Soviet tanks

RIGHT: A recoloured image of a German Sdkfz. 250/11 halftrack, often used in reconnaissance units. This vehicle carried a 28mm Panzerbusche 41 anti-tank gun. (BUNDESARCHIV)

destroyed in four days), the Soviets inflicted damage of their own. Their infantry attached explosive charges to panzers which stopped moving. Some troops even jumped onto panzers to shoot at the crews. German infantry likewise attacked the heavier Soviet tanks with grenades and improvised firebombs when German guns failed to penetrate their armour.

The battle of Dubno ended at the end of June; Between combat losses and mechanical breakdowns, thousands of Soviet tanks littered the region alongside hundreds of German tanks, though many of those could be recovered and repaired. Soviet forces withdrew to reconstitute, having lost most of their tanks and running low on ammunition and fuel. As they withdrew, breakdowns cost even more tanks, left sitting on the sides of roads. Though outnumbering the

Germans, the Soviets simply could not conduct combined arms warfare effectively, while the Germans could. The Red Army had a lot to learn.

For the Germans, their losses were concerning to their leaders, but they resumed their advance. As they neared Kiev they passed the hulks of broken Soviet tanks, many of which never even made it to the battlefield. Gen. Kirponos died in the battle for Kiev in September. Still, each small delay and loss inflicted on the advancing Germans reduced their chance at victory in 1941 and months later they were stopped short of Moscow by Siberian reinforcements and the bitter cold of the Russian winter.

ABOVE: A KV-1 sits in a Ukrainian ditch in July 1941 after the battle. Disabled tanks were usually pushed off the road to clear the way for moving units. No damage is evident, so this tank may simply have broken down. (POLISH ARCHIVES)

LEFT: Two Soviet BA-10 armoured cars sit abandoned and apparently stripped for parts. The BA-10 was well armed but soon replaced in the scouting role by light tanks such as the T-70. (SA-KUVA)

LEFT: 8th Mechanised Corps possessed 48 giant T-35 tanks in June 1941. Only four fought in the battle; the rest broke down en route and two actually fell through bridges. Big but under armoured, the Germans called them 'bogeymen.' (RUSSIAN ARCHIVES)

Outpost Snipe

British determination turns the tide at El Alamein

The war in North Africa saw mechanised armies struggling across the deserts of Egypt and Libya for nearly two years. British Commonwealth and Axis troops battled back and forth as their fortunes, supplies and fuel reserves waxed and waned. By October 1942, after stopping the Axis the previous July at the First Battle of El Alamein, British forces stood ready to push them out of Egypt permanently.

Under the renewed leadership of Lt. Gen. Bernard Montgomery, British Eighth Army stockpiled supplies, replenished tanks and artillery and trained its soldiers for a new offensive. A major role fell to 1st Armoured Division (1AD). It would attack in the area of Kidney Ridge, named for its shape on a map. Nearby was a point codenamed Snipe.

The seizure of Snipe went to 2nd Battalion, The Rifle Brigade (2RB), part of 1AD's infantry component, 7th Motor Brigade. Organised differently from a standard infantry battalion, 2RB possessed scout platoons with 33 tracked Universal Carriers, often known as Bren carriers. There was also a mortar platoon and several machine gun platoons with water-cooled .303 Vickers machine guns.

Significantly, 2RB had S Company, an anti-tank unit with 16 of the new

six-pounder anti-tank guns, a vast improvement over the previous two-pounder. The unit spent the first few days of the battle supporting the engineers clearing the vast minefields laid by Axis forces. By the time it was ordered to seize Snipe, 2RB was down to 76 riflemen and 22 carriers. Fortunately, the battalion received 16 sappers from the 7th Field Squadron

and 239 Battery of the 76th Anti-tank Regiment. This added 11 more six-pounders to their firepower.

2RB's commander, Lt. Col. Victor Turner, received orders to lead his unit to Snipe that night, 26 October, and dig in. A rolling artillery barrage would start on a bearing of 233 degrees five minutes before H-hour, which 2RB was to follow. At dawn, 24 Armoured Brigade would use Snipe as a pivot point for its attack.

Turner instructed his second-in-command, Major Tom Pearson, to prepare 2RB for its mission while Turner went forward to conduct reconnaissance. He saw little but open desert, devoid of terrain features to use for reference. It would be difficult to find the proper point. Unknown to Turner the division's location was off by about 1,000 yards.

The artillery barrage began on time but at a bearing of 270 degrees, so Turner conformed his unit to follow it. The scouts lead the way, followed by the infantry and then the six-pounders, carried by Chevrolet trucks. Lorries with spare ammunition and supplies followed. Scattered enemy fire came in but had no effect.

The column came up to a barbed wire fence, so the engineers checked for mines. Finding none 2RB continued. Dust made it difficult to

LEFT: A six-pounder gun crew in action in the desert. Each shot raised a cloud of dust, revealing its position to the enemy. The camouflage netting draped over the front of the gun was almost useless once the fighting began. (IWM E15560)

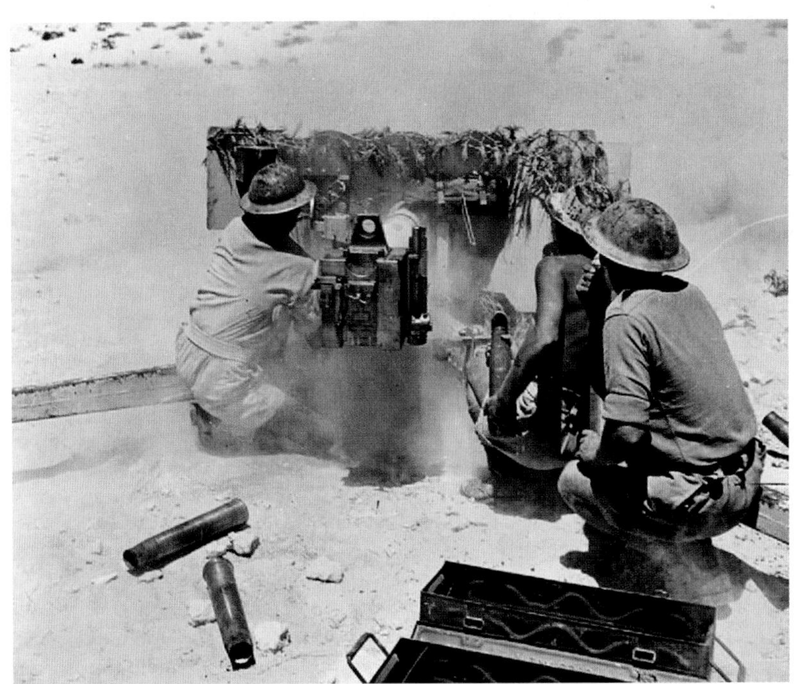

see, and after advancing about 3km Turner asked his artillery Forward Observation Officer (FOO), Capt. Noyes, to ask for a smoke shell to be dropped directly on Snipe. The round landed only 300m away, so Turner thought he was close and moved his unit into an oval-shaped depression about 800 by 400 metres just after midnight on 27 October. The Germans had previously occupied it and a small dugout remained, which Turner used to establish his HQ. Under enemy fire, 2RB set up its guns in an all-round defence and the lorries offloaded the supplies and ammunition and went back for more.

Turner saw campfires around him and he realised he was behind enemy lines. He sent a scouting party west under Lt. Dick Flower. They found two groups of Italian soldiers, who both surrendered. They next discovered an assembly area with 35 German and Italian armoured vehicles. The unit, known as Gruppe Stiffelmayer, failed to notice the British troops, who opened fire with the Bren guns in their carriers. Three supply trucks were set ablaze for the loss of one carrier. Most of the prisoners ran off in the confusion and Flower led his group back to Snipe.

Shortly after, Gruppe Stiffelmayer began moving, perhaps fearing a barrage after being located. One part went north toward a laager of the 15th Panzer Division and the other came straight at Snipe. A Panzer IV F2, with a long, high-velocity 75mm cannon, led the way, but the Germans were unaware of the British unit to their front. The British gunners waited until the panzer was only 30m away and fired. The tank burst into flames. A second six-pounder destroyed a Marder tank destroyer and the rest of the German unit retreated.

The next two hours stayed quiet; the Germans apparently did not realise where the fire had come from. Capt. Noyes went forward to scout for artillery targets and never returned, however, depriving the unit of its FOO.

Shortly after dawn enemy armoured columns began moving through the area, surprisingly headed west. This exposed their side armour to Outpost Snipe so 2RB opened fire. The new six-pounders had no

BELOW: The Sherman was one of Eighth Army's newest and best tanks in late 1942. Though still vulnerable to artillery and anti-tank guns, it had a good blend of firepower, armour and mobility. (IWM E18971)

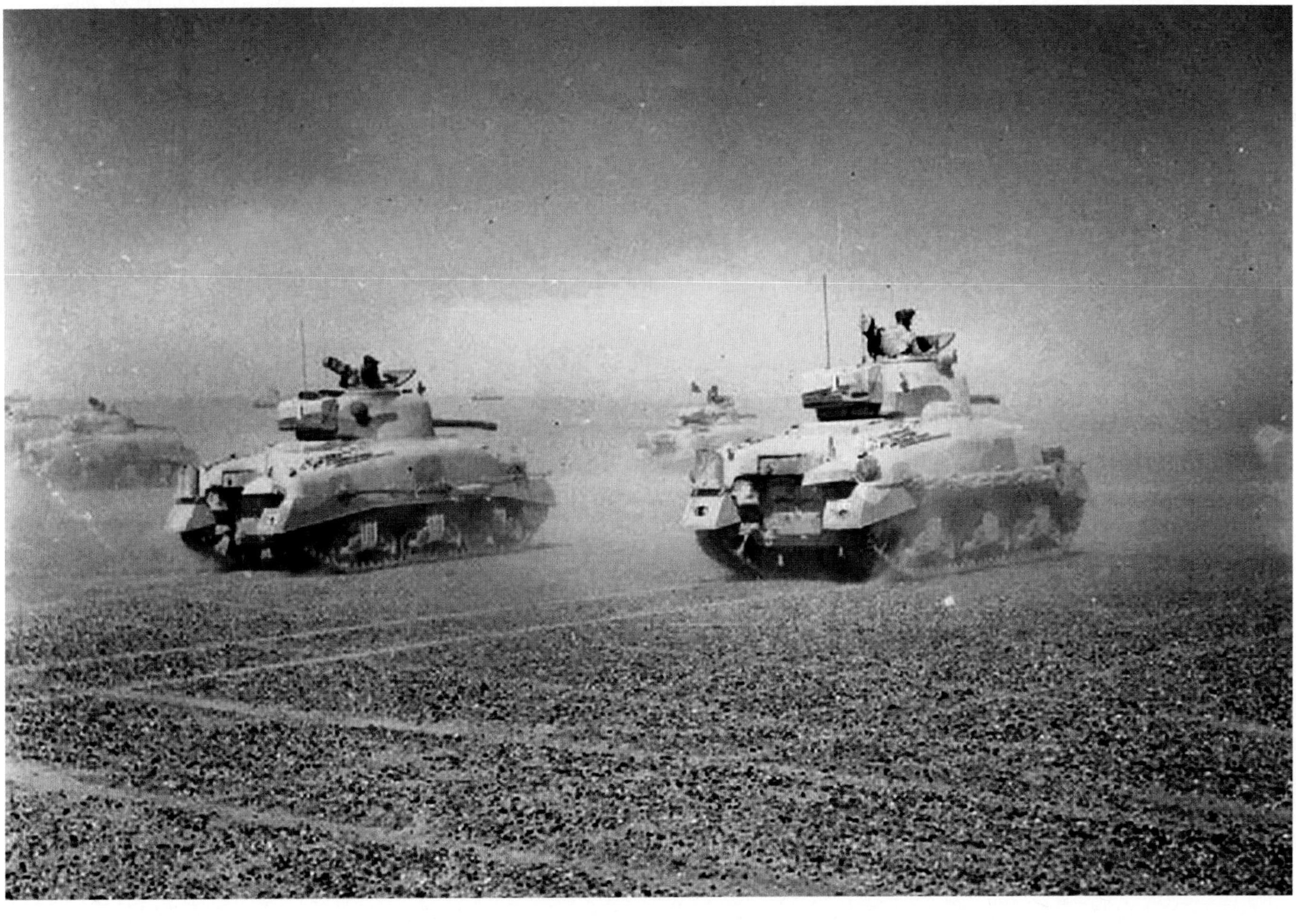

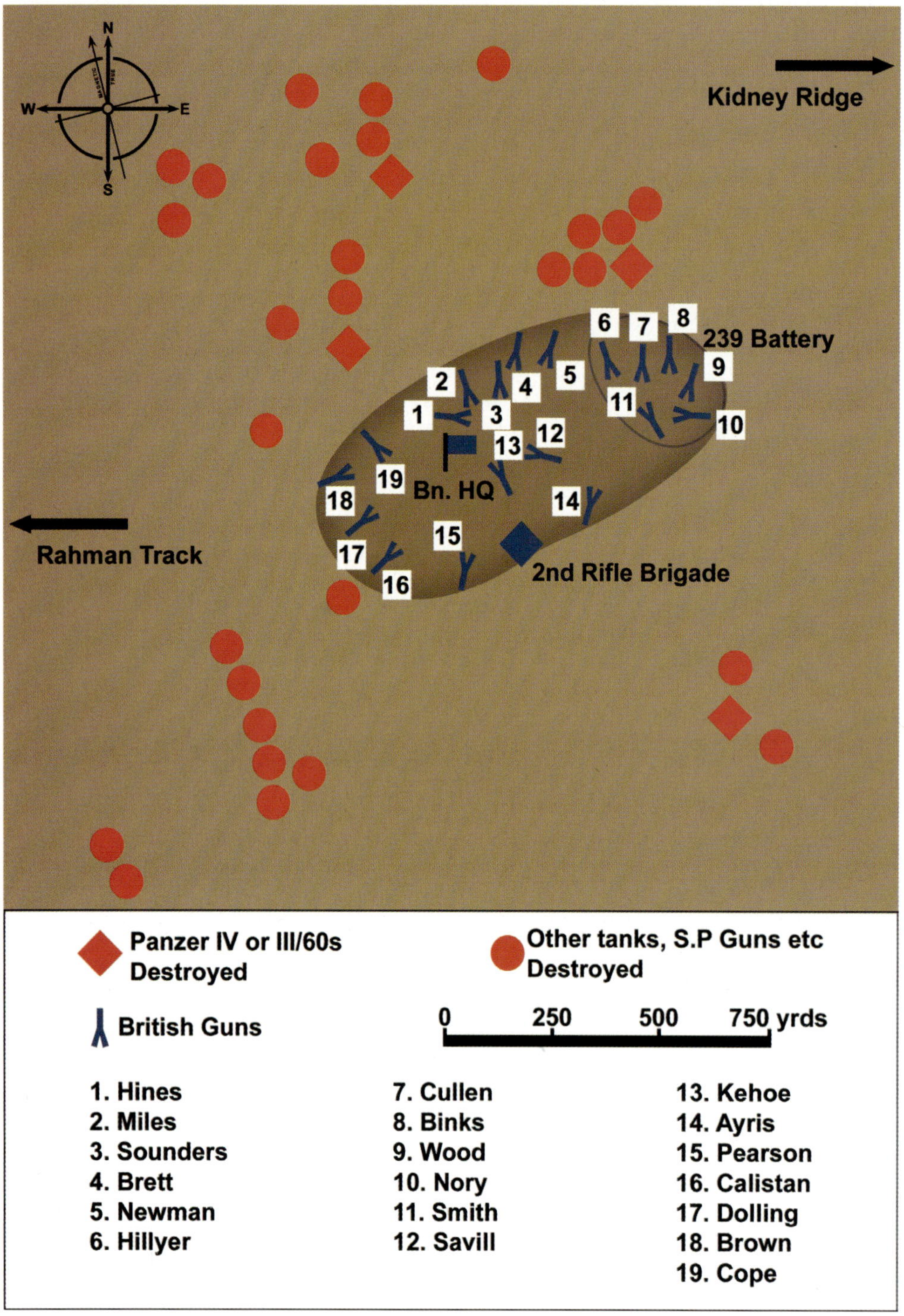
N
W
E
S
Kidney Ridge
239 Battery
Bn. HQ
Rahman Track
2nd Rifle Brigade
Panzer IV or III/60s Destroyed
Other tanks, S.P Guns etc Destroyed
British Guns
0 250 500 750 yrds
1. Hines
2. Miles
3. Sounders
4. Brett
5. Newman
6. Hillyer
7. Cullen
8. Binks
9. Wood
10. Nory
11. Smith
12. Savill
13. Kehoe
14. Ayris
15. Pearson
16. Calistan
17. Dolling
18. Brown
19. Cope

Despite this brave act, the Axis columns were soon retreating, leaving 16 tanks behind. Crewmen from the destroyed vehicles fled on foot across the flat desert. Bursts from Vickers guns cut down many of them. Their position revealed, artillery fire fell on Snipe just as gun crews started relocating their six-pounders to better positions. An officer asked Turner if they were in the correct position; Turner replied, "God knows, but here we are and here we'll stay."

At 0730 AM dust clouds appeared to the east and Sherman tanks of 47RTR appeared on a ridge. Surrounded by the hulks of Axis armour, the British tanks accidentally fired on Snipe, thinking it a German position. It took a half hour to stop the error, but another half hour later the Shermans were hull down within Snipe, just as another German column was seen. Now Snipe drew even more enemy fire. German gunners would spot a British tank and fire a smoke shell to mark its position so other Germans could fire at it. Soon seven Shermans were burning and 47RTR withdrew.

More Axis tanks and infantry gathered around Outpost Snipe and the British grimly resisted. One gunner, Sgt. R. Binks, destroyed a Panzer IV a mile away with three shots. British artillery fire began landing at Snipe but was quickly stopped. Italian infantry gathered for an attack but were scattered by Lt. Flower and his scout platoon in their carriers. The infantry were reduced to their rifles to conserve Vickers ammunition. An officer led three carriers loaded with wounded back to British lines but met intense fire each time they tried to return with ammunition.

Next, 13 Italian tanks led by Capt. Preve attacked, firing as they came. The 2RB gunners quickly destroyed four tanks and forced the rest back. Gruppe Stiffelmayer tried a dual attack against Snipe and 24 Armoured

problem penetrating the panzer's armour even at 800m. One gunner, Sgt. Charles Callistan, said, "I let go at 150 yards. You couldn't miss. All our guns seemed to be firing at once. My target burst into flames but came on for another 50 yards before it halted. Suddenly the night was bright with burning tanks."

An Italian officer, Capitano Preve, described the fight: "Suddenly there is the most violent fire from another eight or ten anti-tank guns hidden on our left and in depth." One of his junior officers led a brave but futile attack. "Second Lieutenant Camplani from outside his turret urges his own tanks to the attack at the head of them, drives his own tank at full speed on the most forward anti-tank gun."

RIGHT: Wounded British soldiers receive treatment at an aid station during the El Alamein fighting. They often had to endure the harsh conditions until they could be evacuated after dark. (IWM)

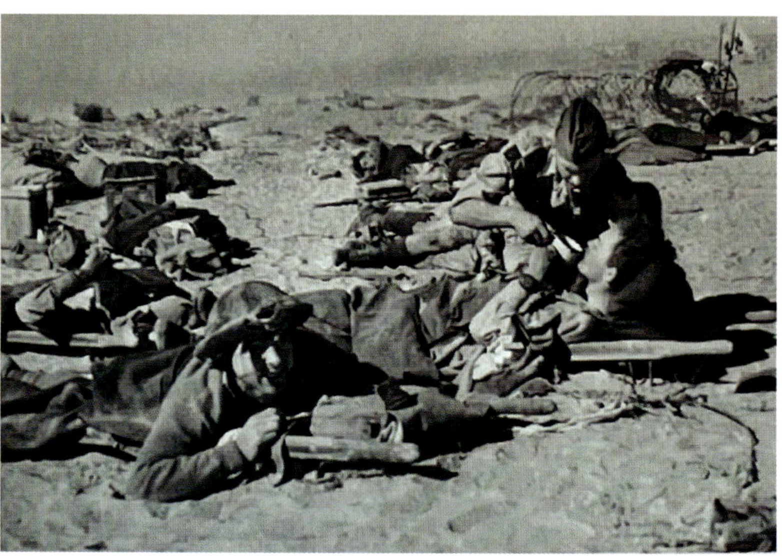

LEFT: The first tank knocked out at Outpost Snipe was a Panzer IV F2 with the long-barrelled 75mm gun. In October 1942 the Afrika Korps had only thirty of these tanks. (US ARMY)

LEFT: A Tommy inspects a partially burnt-out Italian tank. Against the new British six-pounder gun, its armour was entirely inadequate. (IWM E14235)

BELOW: The bane of British armour was the dreaded German FlaK36 88mm gun. This powerful long ranged weapon could destroy any Allied tank. This captured gun has six 'kill rings' painted on the barrel, indicating six enemy tank kills. (IWM E19174)

about 70 armoured vehicles between them, attacked. One column drove past Snipe, however, exposing their side armour. The British waited until they were only 200m away and fired, knocking out several tanks. The rest turned and attacked, but soon a dozen panzers lay burning. The second German column attacked as well, using their machine guns to pin down the British gunners. They waited until the Germans got close and soon destroyed six more tanks, including two Panzer IIIs hit by the same round, which penetrated both tanks. Both German forces retreated. Many of the six-pounders were down to three rounds each.

When another effort to relive Snipe failed, the unit was given permission to withdraw at 11:00PM. 2RB withdrew under fire, with only a few vehicles to carry the wounded and after disabling their guns.

The ordeal of Outpost Snipe was widely retold throughout the British Army. An official inquiry visited the site later and determined 2RB had knocked out 52-57 tanks, up to 20 of which were recovered by the Germans. This constituted about ten percent of Axis tank strength at El Alamein, an amazing result for a single battalion. Lt. Col. Turner received the Victoria Cross for his bravery and leadership while Sgt. Callistan was awarded a Distinguished Service Medal.

A fitting tribute to 2RB's perseverance came from Rommel himself, who wrote "A murderous British fire struck into our ranks and our attack was soon brought to a halt by an immensely powerful anti-tank defence, mainly from dug-in anti-tank guns."

Brigade (24AB) with 25-30 tanks. However, the column aimed at Snipe exposed its flank to 24 AB, while the one attacking 24AB exposed its side to Snipe. Both columns retreated after leaving eight tanks burning.

The Italians returned with eight tanks and an assault gun. Just a single six-pounder under Sgt. Callistan could bear on them and all his crew were wounded. Turner and Lt. Jack Toms ran to help and acted as loaders. Callistan destroyed six vehicles with six shots, but the remaining three kept coming and he had only two rounds left. Turner was wounded in the head but stayed at the gun. Lt. Toms ran to a nearby jeep carrying ammunition. Machine gun fired chased him and even set the jeep on fire, but he arrived with four boxes of ammunition. Callistan destroyed the last three tanks with three shots and used the burning jeep to heat water for tea.

After another friendly artillery fire incident, two more German columns,

The B Company Offensive

US tank destroyers on an independent mission

RIGHT: A posed image of the crew of an M3 Tank Destroyer. The vehicle had impressive anti-tank firepower, but without infantry support, the crew needed to be ready to defend against close attack. (US ARMY)

The first days of the Allied advance into Tunisia were filled with chaos. Anglo-American forces came from the west out of French North Africa after landing there on November 8, 1942. Rommel's Afrika Korps steadily withdrew into Tunisia from the south, pursued by British 8th Army. Meanwhile Axis reinforcements poured into Tunis, in the country's northeast corner.

The American troops were as brave and motivated as they were naïve and inexperienced. They moved into Tunisia unevenly, seeking contact with enemy forces and hoping to cut off Rommel's retreat before he reached Tunis. This poorly coordinated offensive would eventually come to disaster at places like Kasserine Pass. Before that, on occasion American boldness paid off as Axis forces were in equally chaotic circumstances.

RIGHT: An M3's crew layout. The driver and commander sat up front while the gunner, assistant gunner and loader manned the 75mm cannon. (US ARMY)

Company B, 701st Tank Destroyer Battalion (B/701) became one of the first of the new US tank destroyer units to see combat. It had 12 tank destroyers in three platoons of four vehicles each. One platoon employed the M6, a 37mm gun mounted in the bed of a ¾-ton truck. The other two platoons used the M3 tank destroyer, a halftrack mounting a 75mm cannon.

The M6 was obsolete in late 1942, but shortages of better weapons meant some units went into combat with it. The M3 was much more capable but also vulnerable due to its open top and thin armour. The company also had a two-gun antiaircraft section, a 12-man security section for each platoon and an attached reconnaissance platoon.

The company commander, Capt. Gilbert Ellman, completed moving his unit 1,600km from Oran, Algeria to Feriana, Tunisia on November 21, 1942. He immediately received new orders to capture the town of Gafsa, southeast of Feriana, the next morning. They stocked fuel and

RIGHT: An M6 tank destroyer, nicknamed 'Fooey.' Obsolete by late 1942, its underpowered 37mm gun and lack of protection made it dangerous to its crew in action. (US ARMY)

ammunition and set out on a night road march to reach their objective on time. A pair of French armoured cars accompanied them.

Gafsa is a crossroads town with roads leading east, southeast and north. Ellman had no idea if the enemy was even there. He put his M3 platoons in the lead, leaving his more vulnerable M6 platoon at the rear. A pair of P-38 fighters was to strafe the town before B/701's attack. There was no cover on the town's approaches so Ellman decided to use speed, hoping to close the distance before the enemy could mount a defence.

When the P-38s roared over the town, strafing with their cannon and machine guns, B/701 followed behind them, preventing the enemy from having time to reorganise after the air attack. Two clusters of buildings sat on the town's western edge. One platoon moved to each and both immediately took fire from German snipers. They responded by pouring 75mm gunfire into enemy occupied buildings. Most structures collapsed after a single hit.

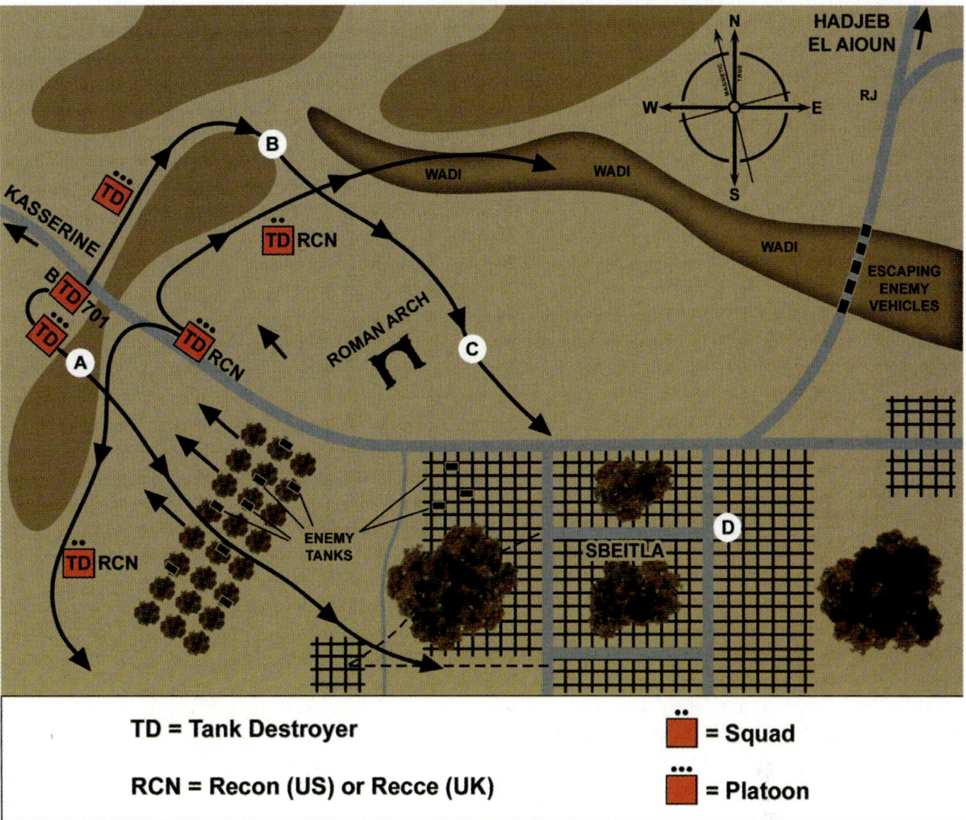

Ellman chose to advance his company to El Guettar, around 15km down the east road, hoping it would prove more suitable.

The scout platoon led, again followed by the M3 platoons. They reached El Guettar without enemy contact. The scouts, mounted in jeeps. continued searching eastward while the tank destroyers dug in. Cresting a small hill just east of town, they saw the German column's tanks coming over a second rise in the distance. The Germans opened fire; in their haste to retreat one of the American drivers flipped his jeep into a ditch. The three occupants were unharmed but had to crawl back to town.

LEFT: German panzers move through a Tunisian town. Most of Tunisia was barren, but most towns had groves of trees which could be used for concealment and cover. (BUNDESARCHIV – CC BY-SA 3.0)

BELOW: A disabled Italian tank in Tunisia. B/701 knocked out several such tanks at Sbeitla using 75mm guns. (US NATIONAL ARCHIVES)

The unit continued into the town, attacking several trench lines dug across and around the road. The French armoured cars stayed on the road and joined the fight against the trenches. Within minutes both were disabled by mines. The Americans moved around the edge of the minefield and entered the town. There, a French boy offered to show them the German positions. The boy lived up to his word and Ellman used cannon and machine gun fire to overcome the enemy infantry.

In less than three hours Gafsa had fallen. Ellman positioned his tank destroyers to guard the approaches to the town. However, he soon learned of a German armoured column approaching from the east. Realising Gafsa was a poor defensive position,

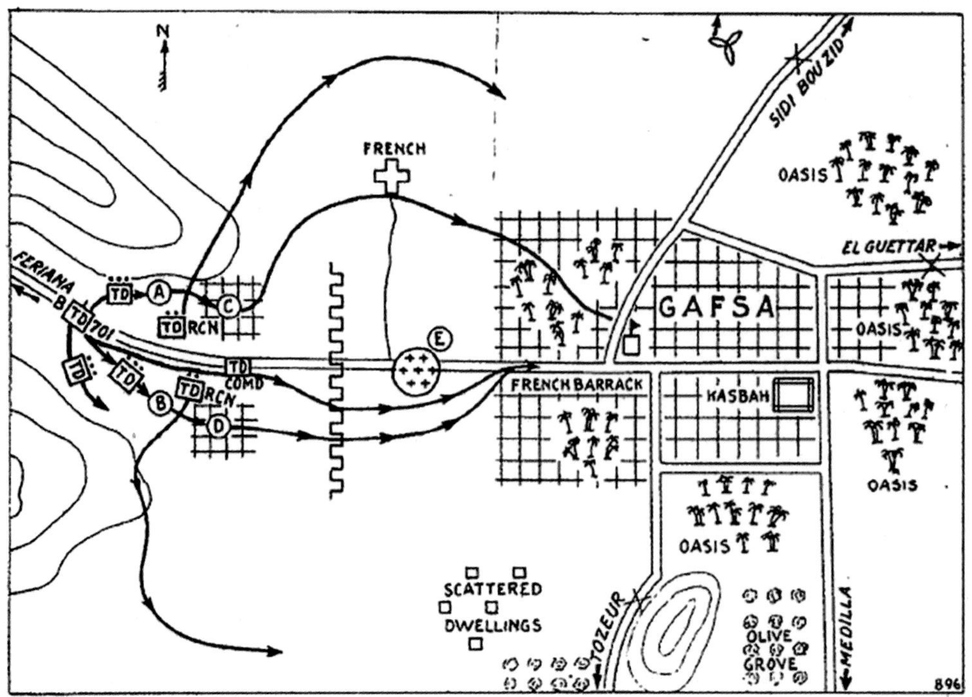

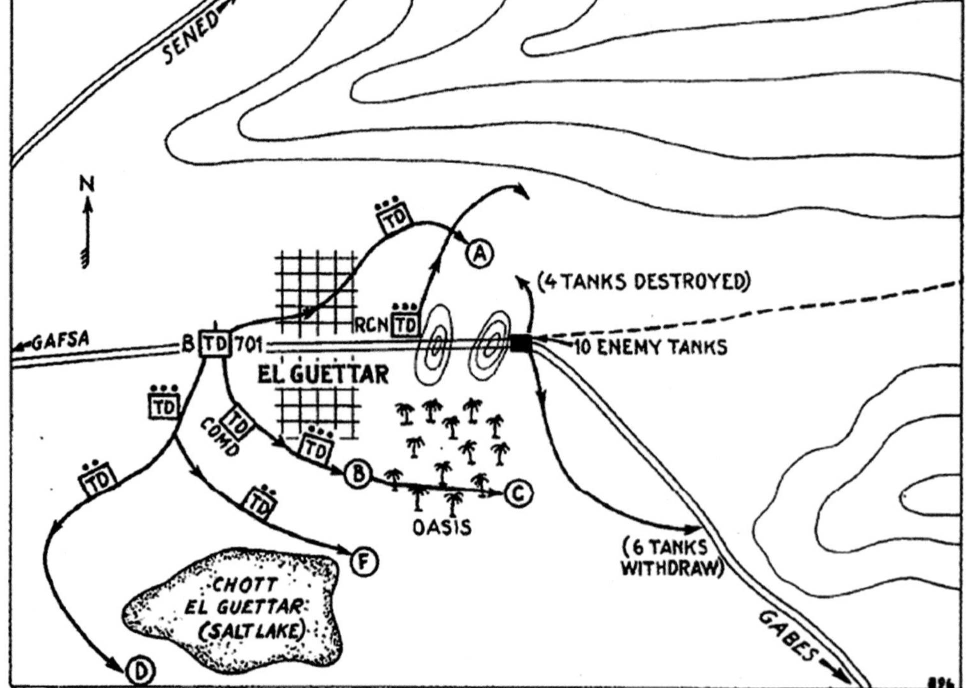

gunners opened fire as well, but all six panzers got past and disappeared up the road. The Americans discovered later several of the panzers were damaged in the short fight and found abandoned a few days later.

With this second success of the day and darkness approaching, Ellman withdrew his unit to Gafsa for maintenance and rest. Upon arriving in Gafsa, he received new orders, however. The town of Sbeitla lay 128km by road north of Gafsa. A German force captured the town from Free French troops earlier in the day. Ellman's success had earned his company a reputation for getting the job done; now the French commander wanted the American unit to go to Sbeitla and 'do something about it.' Ellman later noted such vague orders were common in the early days in Tunisia.

The mission carried risk, requiring a night road march through unsecured areas followed by an attack against an enemy force of unknown size. Still, B/701 was the only unit available, so they topped off their fuel tanks and drove to Feriana, leaving behind the M6 platoon to help secure Gafsa. At Feriana they stopped for two hours of sleep before continuing to Sbeitla.

They advanced more cautiously, with the scouts told to be especially thorough. One M3 of the lead platoon went with them in case they ran into trouble. The crew of the M3 kept a round in the chamber of their 75mm gun, ready to fire at a moment's notice. When they reached the town of Kasserine, locals told them the Germans had been there but fallen back to Sbeitla.

Continuing, the scouts found a roadblock about 8km outside Kasserine, stones piled on the road in the saddle between two hilltops. It was perfect obstacle for an enemy ambush, so the scouts approached

TOP: The American commander's handmade maps of B/701's actions. Here, Gafsa.

ABOVE: El Guettar

Aware of the enemy, Ellman placed his M3 platoons with one on each side of the road. The M6 platoon went around a salt marsh south of town to cover the company's flank. The German force, with 10 tanks, flanked the town to their right, bringing them directly into the path of the platoon Ellman deployed on his left.

The American platoon fired first, slamming 75mm armour-piercing rounds into the German tanks. Within moments four were knocked out and the remaining six fell back. As the Germans retreated, they unwittingly moved past the second platoon, which had set up in an oasis just south of the road. These

RIGHT: A US artillery crew fires their howitzer, mounted in a half track. The M3 tank destroyer had a similar setup and crew positions. (US ARMY)

slowly, probing for enemy positions. They found nothing. Inexplicably, the roadblock was not defended or even booby-trapped. The Americans cleared it and resumed their advance.

After moving another 16km, they came to a wrecked bridge and had to find another crossing point. Nearing Sbeitla, they expected to approach it from the southwest, but their maps were wrong. Cresting a north-south ridge, the scouts found Sbeitla in front of them; the road came into town from the northwest. An orchard sat on the western edge of town, with an old Roman arch on the north side of the road. Another road led northeast out of town, crossing a wadi.

No fire greeted the scouts as they approached. They later learned the Italian garrison was eating lunch when the Americans arrived, neglecting to post sentries. Their luck ran out when an Italian tank crewman spotted the Americans and sounded the alarm. Camouflaged tanks and machine guns in the orchard opened fire. The US scouts replied with their own machine guns, including a .50-calibre Browning on the scout platoon leader's halftrack, covering the jeep's withdrawal. The attached M3 sent 75mm shells into the orchard.

Reaching the ridge, Ellman sent one platoon to flank Sbeitla from the north while the other platoon set up a base of fire against the orchard. He divided the scout platoon's jeeps between them so they could add the firepower of their machine guns. The machine gunners kept the Italian tank crews buttoned up in their vehicles, reducing their visibility. They also revealed the tank's locations to the American gunners when the machine gun's tracer bullets bounced off the armour into the air.

With the Italian armour pinned, the flanking platoon bounded to the Roman arch and opened fire. Several enemy tanks were destroyed

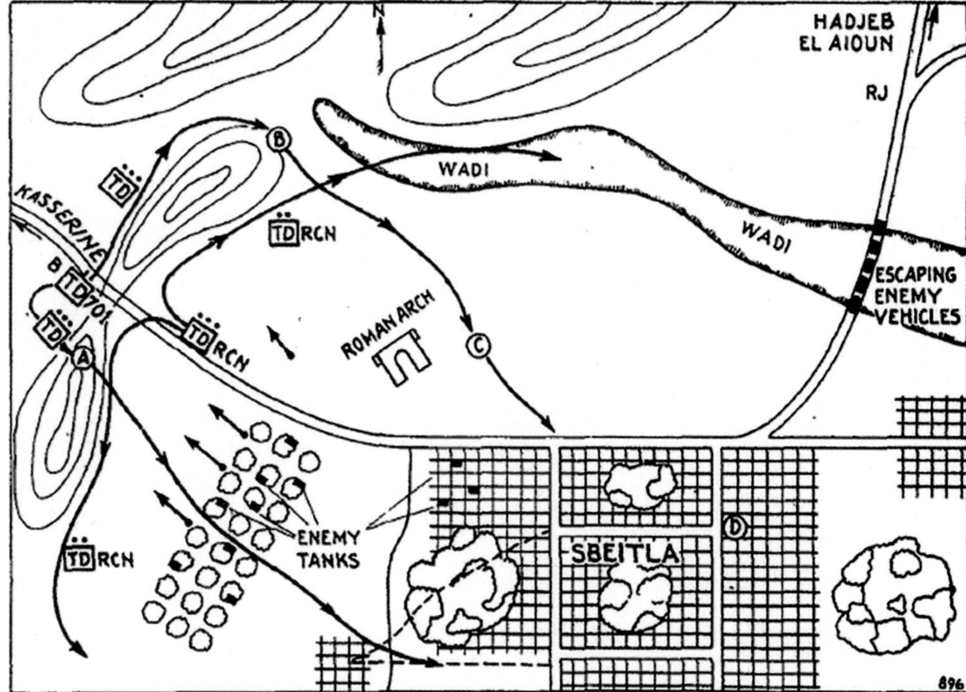

ABOVE: Sbeitla

LEFT: US and French troops inspect a knocked out Italian tank. The thin armour on Italian tanks made them vulnerable to most Allied anti-tank weapons. (US NATIONAL ARCHIVES)

and more were knocked out in the crossfire as the rest retreated from the orchard. The enemy force actually consisted of Germans and Italians. The Germans, seeing the battle was going against them, decided to withdraw. They left using the northeast road, the surviving Italian tanks following them. One M3 crew tried to cut off their escape but heavy machine gun fire disabled the M3 and wounded one crewman, the only casualty B/701 took in their two-day offensive. The rest of the Axis troops made good their escape and Ellman secured the town until a French unit arrive to defend it.

During their two days of operations, B/701 destroyed 15 tanks and took 400 prisoners while moving 650km. In return they suffered one wounded and damage to two vehicles. The towns they took would all change hands at least once during the rest of the Tunisian campaign. Once the lines solidified, such attacks became more costly, but in the fluid situation of mid-November 1942, B/701's speed and daring paid off.

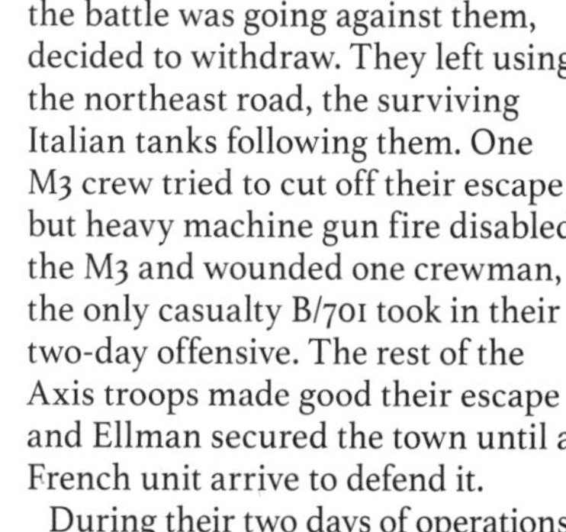

LEFT: An Italian Semovente self-propelled gun with German and Italian staff cars. The Germans considered it one of the more effective Italian armoured vehicles. (BUNDESARCHIV BILD 101I-784-0208-17A)

ABOVE: American officers inspect a French Renault R35 tanks after hostilities ended. Its low-velocity short-barrelled 37mm had poor armour penetration and it was easily defeated even by the outdated M3 Stuart. (US ARMY)

The Battle of Happy Valley

The US Army's first tank battle with Nazi Germany

The US Army entered the war in North Africa in November 1942, coming ashore in French North Africa and subsequently advancing east as part of an Anglo-American offensive into Tunisia. The Americans were raw and inexperienced, but also eager and aggressive. They had to learn hard lessons about modern combat, a deadly curriculum the British army spent nearly three years learning.

The 1st Battalion, 1st Armored Regiment (1/1) of the US 1st Armored Division became an armored unit in July 1940. It shipped to the UK in May 1942 before subsequent assignment to Operation Torch, the invasion of French North Africa. Lt. Col. John Waters, son-in-law of General George Patton, commanded the battalion.

Standard organisation for a US tank regiment at the time was one battalion of M3 light tanks and two of M3 or M4 medium tanks. 1/1 used the M3 light, commonly known by the British-applied name Stuart, though American tank crews rarely used it

at the time. The M3 carried a 37mm cannon, obsolete by this point in the war, and its armour was at best 51mm thick. The tank was reliable, fast and agile; despite its weaknesses, its crews tried to undertake the same tasks as their medium tank-equipped cohorts.

The battalion went ashore with the first wave of troops at Oran, Algeria on November 8, 1942, because the landing craft available could not carry the larger medium tanks. Their first order tasked them to seize Tafaraoui airfield, ten miles south of the city.

RIGHT: This aged image shows a US Army M3 Stuart in Tunisia in 1942. The large American flag was used during the Operation Torch landings in hopes of preventing combat with Vichy French forces, who might be unwilling to fight Americans. (US ARMY)

The lead unit was B Company under Captain William Tuck. Their arrival prevented Vichy French aircraft from interfering with the landings. The French defenders opened fire on them with anti-aircraft guns, but their weapons could not depress far enough to hit the diminutive M3s. After a short, mild fight, the French surrendered. Tuck recalled, "We considered it intense at the time... we had a lot to learn."

The next day aerial reconnaissance spotted a French armoured column moving on the airfield from the south. Ordered to intercept, I/I moved south, Capt. Tuck's company again in the lead. They found French Renault R35 tanks taking up defensive positions atop a small hill. Tuck ordered one platoon of M3s to lay down a base of fire while the other two platoons flanked to the French right. French rounds bounced of the M3's armour, but the American fired penetrated. Soon 14 French tanks were knocked out, some afire.

Many of the men were pleased at their victories over the French, but Waters knew the battle-hardened Germans would be tougher opponents. He told them, "We did very well against the scrub team. Next week we hit German troops. Do not slack off in anything. When we make

a showing against them you may congratulate yourselves."

Soon after, I/I moved to Tunisia becoming part of an advance trying to cut of the retreat of Rommel and his Afrika Korps from Libya into Tunisia. Allied intelligence thought the Germans were evacuating as fast as they could. Instead, reinforcements were pouring in and preparing to fight.

As I/I moved east it came under sporadic air attack and learned to spread out its formations. Along the roads, British engineers had placed signs: "Don't sit and die- jump and run." Arriving at Beja, Waters reported for his orders, which were vague. He was told to create a 'tank infested area' around the Chouigui Pass, which connected the Tine River Valley of northern central Tunisia to the Plain of Tunis. He received no explanation as to how he should "infest" the area with tanks; there was a sense, however, the area was a weak spot in the Axis line. The difficulties were many; air and artillery support were almost non-existent, save for the battalion's own mortars and howitzer-toting halftracks. Likewise, there was no infantry support, a severe limitation for an armoured unit, which depended on infantry to protect against enemy anti-tank guns.

The battalion moved out the next day, 25 November 1942, advancing alongside a British armoured regiment. Rugged hills surrounded the Chouigui Pass, soon renamed 'Chewy-Gooey' pass by the American troops. A road led down the pass east toward the town of Tebourba. Waters assigned Company A, under Major Carl Siglin, to hold the west end of the pass against any German advance from the battalion's rear. B Company, under now-Major Tuck (All the company commanders were promoted after Oran) would hold the eastern end of the pass facing Tebourba. Major Rudolph Barlow, the C Company commander, would take his tanks on a reconnaissance east of the pass.

As the companies readied to deploy, two Italian tanks came down the road south from Mateur, apparently scouting for the Americans. M3s from the battalion command >

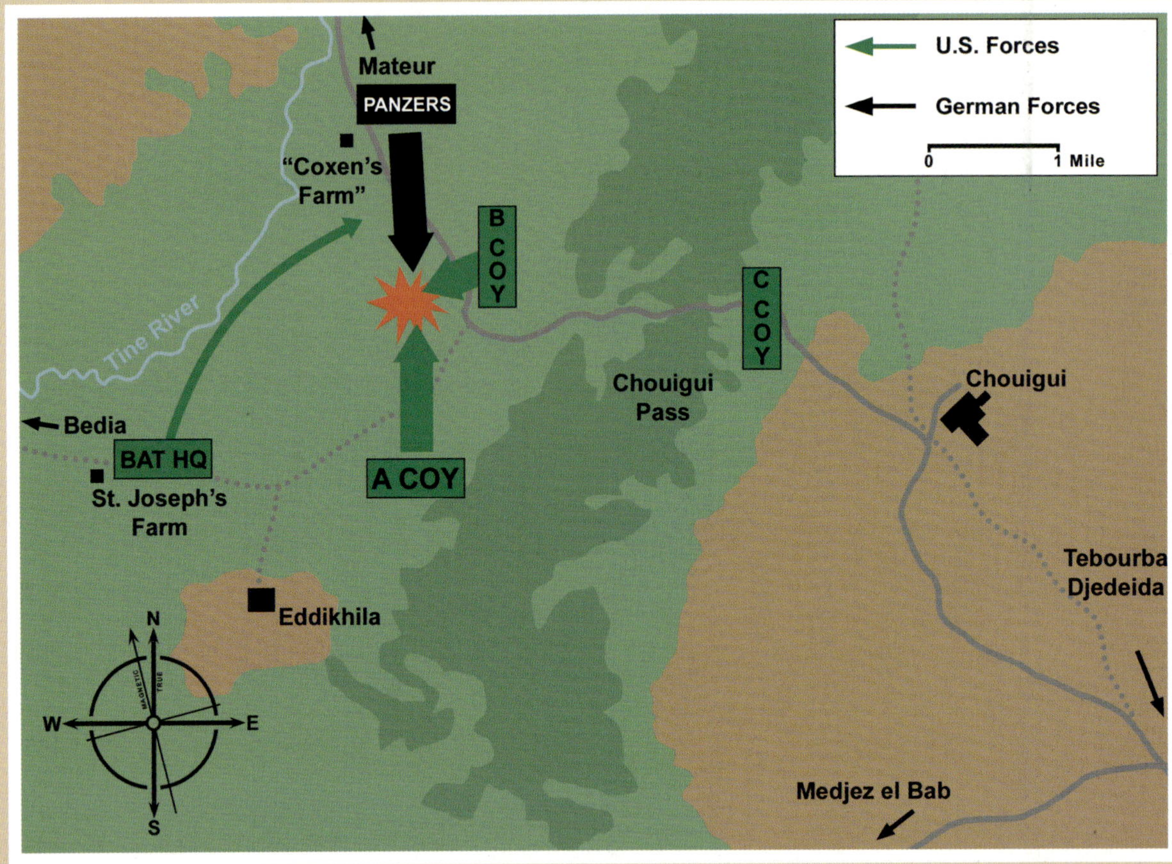

BELOW: A unit of M3s on desert exercises before Operation Torch. In action, American tank crews soon learned to spread out their formation to lessen losses from artillery and air attacks. (US ARMY)

section quickly destroyed them. The Americans also found a German-occupied farmhouse 2km north along the Mateur Road. Waters ordered A Company to attack it, but not to become so heavily engaged it could not defend the west end of the pass. The farm complex was well fortified, with a stout wall, and the German had a few anti-tank guns. The battle resulted in the Americans losing one tank with another disabled in return for destroying the anti-tank guns. The Americans shelled it with their 75mm howitzer-equipped halftracks and pulled back, leaving the Germans in possession of the complex.

The Germans must have called for help; quickly a mixed force of fighters and light bombers attacked A Company, killing one and wounding several. After the attack, the Americans named the area 'Happy Valley.' Meanwhile, C Company set out on its reconnaissance. Waters ordered its commander to check on two bridges near Tebourba and authorised him to engage any enemy forces, if practical. Major Barlow took this authorisation to heart.

Moving east down the pass, C Company first encountered several German scout cars coming west. These were quickly destroyed and the column of M3s continued on the town of Chouigui, at the eastern mouth of the pass. The Americans rushed in, completely surprising a German reconnaissance company. Machine gun and cannon fire from the tanks cut through the Germans. Bodies and wrecked vehicles littered the town.

Continuing east, they reached the first bridge and overcame its German guards. The next bridge sat five miles toward Tebourba, so the Americans sped on, one platoon scouting ahead. Reaching a small ridge, the tankers were surprised to find a German airfield with dozens of aircraft

LEFT: The force that 1/1 met at Chouigui Pass was likely a mixed group of tank types, such as this Panzer III. An ammunition explosion is probably responsible for the missing turret roof. (IWM NA386)

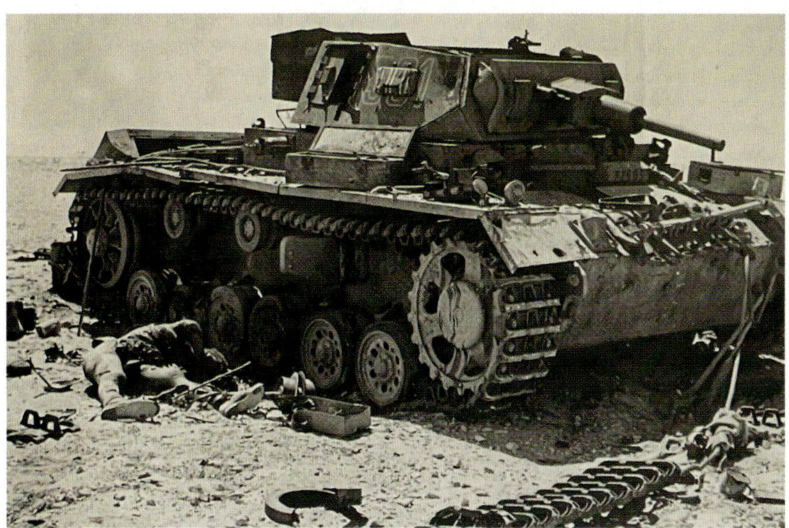

spread out before them on the plain below. Ironically, these were the same planes which had attacked them earlier.

Maj. Barlow put his tanks on line and charged as if they were horse cavalry, causing chaos among the Germans below. Cannon and machine gun fire poured from each tank, riddling enemy planes where they sat. A few tankers took their M3s and physically crushed the tails of fighters under their treads. One tank quickly moved to the end of the runway and put a round of canister into any German plane trying to take off. They soon destroyed 36 aircraft and shot up the hangers and fuel supplies. Barlow later received a British Military Cross for this action.

After their success, C Company was ordered back to the east end of the pass. A Company occupied a hill south of the west end of the pass while B Company took up a similar position immediately to their north. The next morning 1/1 spotted a German column moving south from Mateur. They saw long booms extending from the vehicles and thought it was an engineer unit; actually, the 'booms' were the long barrels of Panzer IV F2 tanks, not yet encountered by the Americans.

The Germans spotted the Americans and attacked. The battalion's howitzer section fired 30 rounds at the panzers to no effect before being forced back by enemy fire. Siglin ordered A Company to attack the German force, which had a few Italian armoured vehicles with it.

The Americans quickly destroyed an Italian light tank before turning their fire on the panzers, who were still in column on the road. The Germans quickly turned and attacked, leaving several M3s burning. The M3s kept firing but their rounds simply bounced off the frontal armour of the panzers. The German fire went right through, and soon six M3s sat wrecked.

Critically, the Germans did not spot B Company, which stayed hidden until the Germans turned to attack A Company, presenting their thinly armoured rears. One American shot hit just behind a panzer's rear drive sprocket, starting a fire. Knowledge of this weak spot spread and soon more German tanks burned; between four and nine were destroyed before the Germans withdrew.

Tactically, the battle was a draw, with both sides taking losses. However, the Americans still held the pass and managed to fend off a superior German force. Through daring, 1/1 had inflicted serious losses in troops, armour and aircraft on the Germans. They also learned of shortcomings in their weapons and tactics. The Americans began to learn valuable lessons they would need in the coming weeks and months.

BELOW: Italian tanks were obsolete by late 1942 but often continued in service as reconnaissance vehicles. American tanks destroyed several of them at Chouigui Pass. This M14/41 is on display at the Tank Museum in Bovington. (AUTHOR'S COLLECTION)

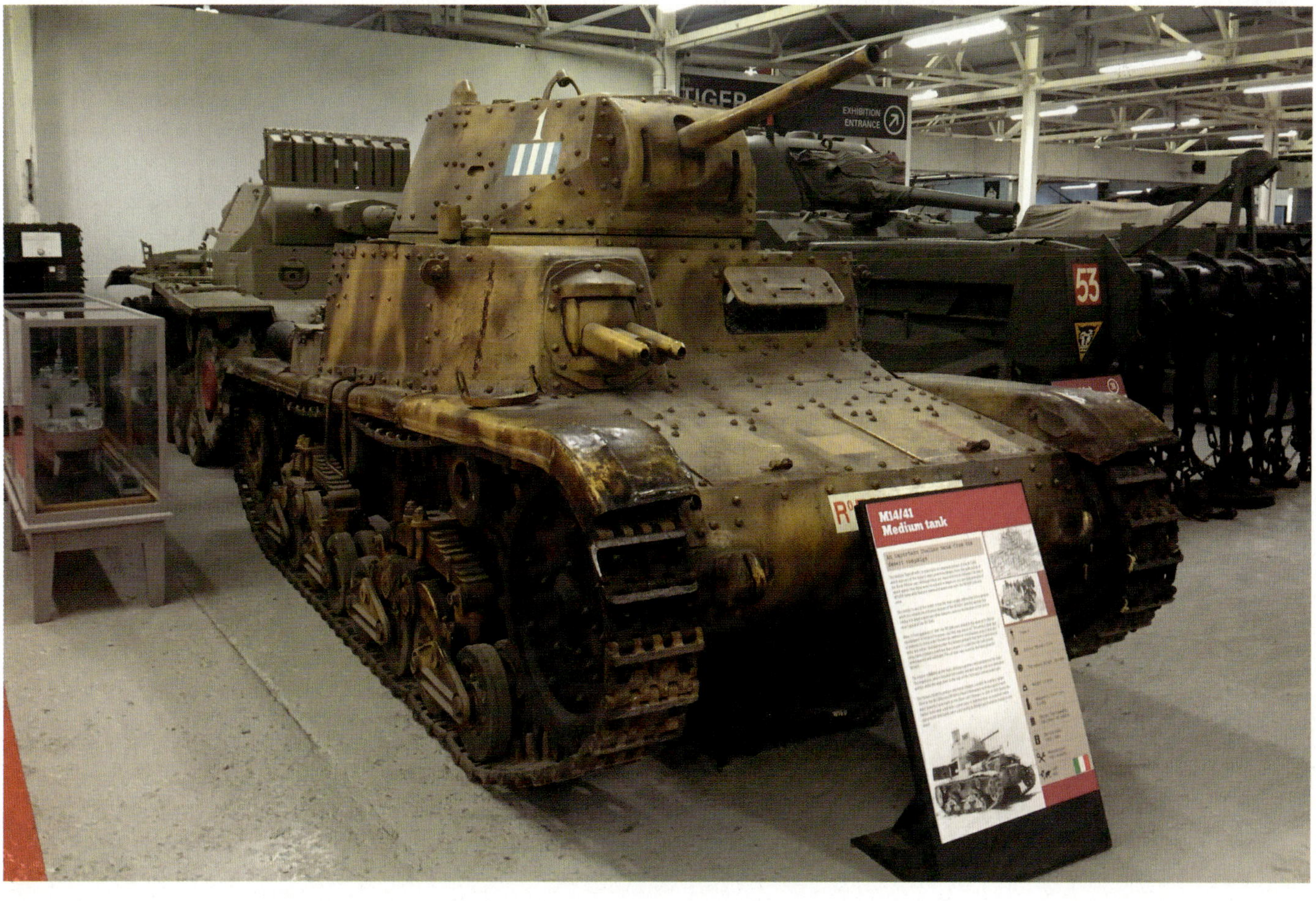

Captain Hollands' One-Tank Offensive

As the German lost ground in Tunisia in February 1943, they launched a desperate offensive called Operation Ochsenkopf (Oxhead) to reverse their waning fortunes. One column of this attack cut the road between El Aroussa and Medjez el Bab, southwest of Tunis. It ran into a unit of the North Irish Horse and was defeated, retreating to a large agricultural complex known as Steamroller Farm, named simply for the large steamroller which sat in the open near the farm's buildings.

The next morning Maj. E.W.H. Hadfield, commanding A Squadron 51 Royal Tank Regiment received orders to scout the area the following day; his superiors were "concerned about the valley north of El Aroussa as a result of previous action and wished a recce [reconnaissance] in force from El Aroussa up to the farm… to find what German tanks were in the valley and to clear up any enemy infantry in the gullies."

Hadfield's squadron used the Churchill tank, large and slow but well armoured and tough, equipped with a six-pounder gun for which they had only armour-piercing (AP) ammunition. Supporting the tanks were a company of infantry from 2 Coldstream Guards and a few 25-pounder guns. A Squadron's strength stood at 13 Churchills in four troops with two or three tanks each. Each tank's name began with the letter 'A.'

Little was known of the area when Hadfield's force set out on 28 February, the infantry riding on the tanks. The British believed some infantry with a few tanks and anti-tank guns defended the farm. In actuality, two battalions of the Hermann Goering Division with heavy anti-tank support defended the area.

The advance went slowly and methodically, watching out for German ambushes. When the British reached the farm, the road bottlenecked with rough ground all around it. Hadfield knew this was a good spot for an ambush and deployed his force, sending 2 and 3 Troops (five tanks) to the left to avoid the bad ground. Troops 1 and 4 moved below the farm and took up hull-down positions to support the infantry when they approached the farm.

Soon after Hadfield ordered 1 Troop (two tanks) to move up the road. Captain Earnest Hollands led the troop, his tank named Adventurer. A former police officer and enlisted soldier raised from the ranks, Hollands had a reputation for bravery. The clank of the Churchill's tracks mixed with the roar of their Bedford engines as they advanced toward Steamroller Farm.

As 1 Troop rolled slowly uphill, they spotted several anti-tank guns

ABOVE: A group of Churchills moving across a Tunisian landscape in 1943. The closest tank is an older model with a two-pounder gun in the turret and a 3-inch howitzer mounted in the hull. (IWM)

hidden in gullies. Both tanks opened fire, driving the crews away from their weapons until the infantry caught up. The entire squadron then opened fire on the farm complex to suppress any enemy troops there. Afterward the infantry advanced to clear the buildings. Hadfield ordered the squadron to advance through the farm to the next ridge.

As they moved, a squadron of Ju-87 Stukas appeared and commenced dive-bombing. Simultaneously, multiple German antitank guns opened fire. A wadi separated the Churchills from their antagonists and at least one gun was an 88mm, able to pierce even the Churchill's thick armour. The German fire disabled four tanks, setting one afire, but in return the British silenced several anti-tank guns and mortar positions. The battle soon stalemated.

Hadfield reported the action and received an order to take the farm and the ridge beyond 'at all costs.' Success would help make the German position in the area untenable. Still, fully one-third of his tanks were out of action. He decided to order only 1 Troop forward and save his remaining tanks for

whatever happened next. Hadfield knew the decision was unfair to Hollands, but in the brutal logic of war it made sense, as enemy strength was unknown. In the heat of combat, he forgot that 1 Troop had lost one of its two tanks already. Hollands crew would advance alone.

Hollands received the order without complaint and told his driver, Trooper John Mitton, to advance. Adventurer

LEFT: Captain Ernest Hollands served in the British Army in India before the war and earned a Distinguished Conduct Medal at Dunkirk in 1940 for rescuing a downed German pilot from his burning plane. (IWM)

moved to the road, the only place to cross the wadi. Enemy shells soared around them. The tank crawled forward, the crew alert.

Moving around a curve in the road, they ran into an 88mm gun only 30m away. Mitton stopped the tank so the gunner could fire accurately. Fire from the machine guns and six-pounder wrecked the enemy gun before it could fire. The farm sat to their left, so Hollands ordered the turret traversed that way as Adventurer moved ahead, soon arriving at a barrier of branches across the road. Suddenly they realised the barrier concealed another 88. Their turret turned to the left, only the hull machine gunner, Trooper Hank Howsen, could engage, but he was reloading his Besa machine gun.

The German gun fired, the AP round crossing the distance in a fraction of a second. Amazingly, it struck the top of the turret, cutting a deep gouge but leaving the tank operational. The Germans reloaded as Adventurer's gunner rotated the turret, but a six-pounder round had come loose from the ammunition rack and jammed the turret. Hollands reached for his Thompson submachine gun as the ➲

BELOW: Dust rises from the ground as a Churchill fires its six-pounder gun in Tunisia. Churchills were slow, reaching only 8 mph cross country, but several of them took repeated hits from anti-tank guns and remained operational. (IWM)

Germans fired again, but they missed completely. Howsen finished loading his weapon and fired a burst, sending the German crew running. Mitton drove the tank forward as Hollands threw grenades at the Germans.

Moving past the two destroyed 88s, Hollands spotted a bit of high ground with some pine trees and decided to move there. Once near the summit, he saw an opportunity laid out before him. A large enemy vehicle laager sat across the road, with dozens of trucks, staff and scout cars, even another 88mm gun with its tractor and ammunition lorry. About three companies of infantry dotted the area, many sitting in slit trenches. Hollands did not waste a second; he ordered his crew to open fire.

Round after round of six-pounder shot tore into the enemy vehicles. Some burst into flame as troops scattered for cover. Howsen's Besa machine gun chattered, adding to the cacophony of sound and fury unleashed on the nearly defenceless Germans. Within a few minutes 25 vehicles were reduced to wreckage. Hollands radioed Hadfield to report

ABOVE: A German Panzer III tank knocked out in Tunisia. Trooper Nicholson in Lt. Renton's tank destroyed two such tanks at Steamroller Farm. The hulks remained there days later. (US NATIONAL ARCHIVES)

RIGHT: The rough terrain around Steamroller Farm provided good cover for German infantry and anti-tank guns, but the Churchill tank's ability to cross such ground surprised them (IWM)

RIGHT: A tank of 51 RTR in Tunisia, next to a Universal Carrier. Here, the Churchill's effective six-pounder gun and two Besa machine guns are in view. This tank has lost one of its track covers, which were often knocked off in action. (IWM)

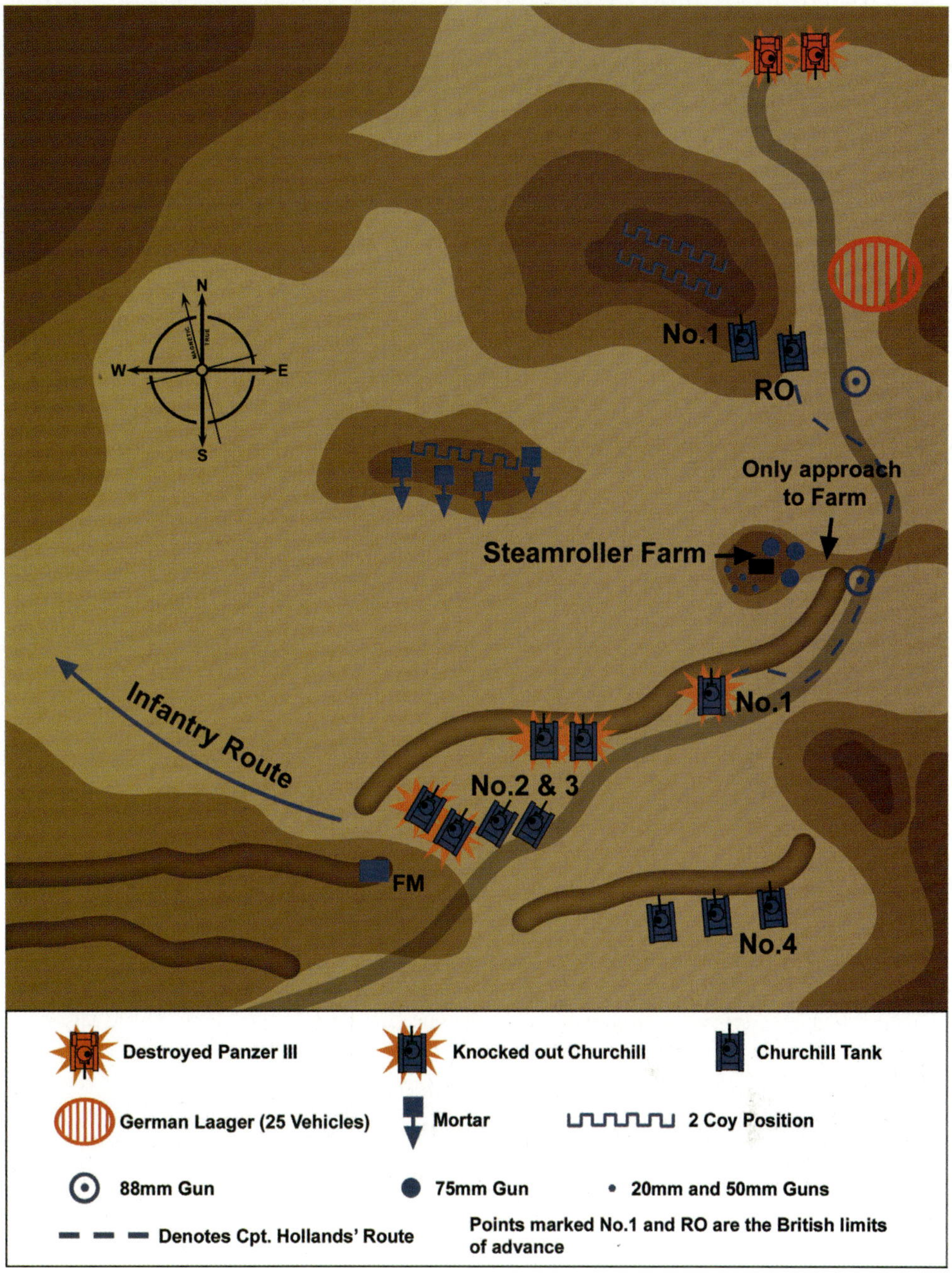

and ask for help, as he knew the Germans would quickly reconstitute and counterattack.

The fighting around the farm still raged, leaving Hadfield with little to spare. The only tank he could send belonged to Lt. J. Renton, the squadron reconnaissance officer. Renton wasted no time and set out along Hollands' route. He soon passed the knocked out 88s and kept going.

Meanwhile, Adventurer fought a duel with a lone German soldier, who fired rifle grenades at the Churchill from a nearby slit trench. Three six-pounder rounds and two full belts of machine gun ammunition failed to stop their attacker. Finally, the gunner took careful aim and sent a cannon round into the dirt in front of the slit trench, causing an explosion which covered the trench in smoke and dust. When it cleared, the German rose from the trench, stunned. He looked at Adventurer a moment and then slowly turned around, dropped his rifle and staggered away. They could have shot him, but the British crew let him go.

Renton reached the high ground, stopping his tank near Adventurer. His arrival proved fortuitous, as two Panzer III tanks appeared a few hundred meters away. Adventurer could not depress its gun far enough to engage, but Renton's tank could. The gunner, Trooper Nicholson, put three AP rounds into each tank, destroying them.

Hadfield ordered both tanks to return to the squadron; the farm was too well-defended to take that day. Going back the way they came, Adventurer stopped to put a few AP rounds into the camouflaged 88 to prevent its recovery. The engine stalled and would not restart. Renton directed his tank around to Adventurer's front and the crew attached a tow cable. German mortar and machine gun fire fell all around them as they worked. Once Renton's tank began pulling, Adventurer's engine started and both tanks kept

Destroyed Panzer III

Knocked out Churchill

Churchill Tank

German Laager (25 Vehicles)

Mortar

2 Coy Position

88mm Gun

75mm Gun

20mm and 50mm Guns

Denotes Cpt. Hollands' Route

Points marked No.1 and RO are the British limits of advance

going. Along the way they picked up the crew of a burning Churchill.

The battle at Steamroller Farm cost the British five tanks, though two were later recovered. Worse,

they suffered three dead and 11 wounded. Hollands' squadron mates did not believe his report, but a few days later, when the British took the area, the remains showed even more damage than Hollands reported. The Germans lost eight anti-tank guns, 25 wheeled vehicles, and the two panzers. Mortars and anti-aircraft guns lay wrecked, with between 150 to 200 dead Germans. British signallers also intercepted a German radio message, claiming the British attacked with "a mad tank battalion which scaled impossible heights."

Capt. Hollands received a Distinguished Service Order, while Lt. Renton was awarded a Military Cross. Trooper Mitton received a Military Medal. Hollands' war ended in 1944 when he was wounded in Italy, but he returned to Bath and rejoined the police service.

LEFT: A late-model Panzer III. This model served as the mainstay of German tank forces in North Africa. (BUNDESARCHIV)

Panzer Killers at El Guettar

A US Tank Destroyer battalion faced the 10th Panzer Division

RIGHT: Officers of the 601st study a map during the battle on March 23. Note the M3 in the background, using the terrain as cover. (US ARMY)

As the fighting in Tunisia raged on, the US Army was learning its lessons in a very harsh tutelage. General George Patton now commanded the US II Corps and got his troops back on their feet after the defeat at Kasserine Pass. In March 1943 Patton received orders to advance from El Guettar down Highway 15 to both draw some Axis troops away from the Mareth line, where British 8th Army was fighting, and to break through to the sea, cutting Axis-held territory in two.

On 23 March, the US Army's 1st Infantry Division (1ID) prepared to spearhead that attack, but the Germans struck first. Sensing the threat an advance from El Guettar posed, they launched a spoiling attack using 10th Panzer Division, with 57 serviceable tanks and a like number of other armoured vehicles. Such a unit could do great damage to even an infantry division.

Fortunately, 1ID had an attached tank destroyer battalion, the 601st, under Lt. Col. H.D. Baker. On 23 March the unit had 31 M3 tank destroyers available, in three companies designated A, B, and C. The M3 halftracks carried a powerful 75mm gun, effective against any Axis tank in Tunisia, except the rarely seen Tiger. They were thinly armoured and open-topped, however, leaving the crews vulnerable to incoming fire.

BELOW: Many of the German tanks at El Guettar were Panzer IVs with the long 75mm high-velocity cannon. This example is at the Tank Museum at Bovington. (AUTHOR)

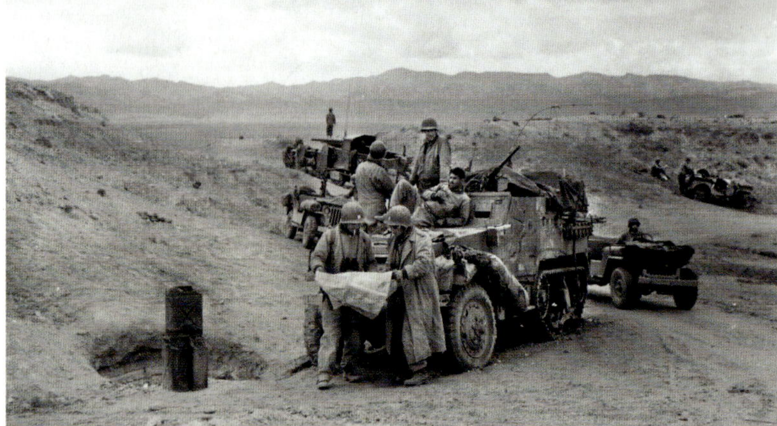

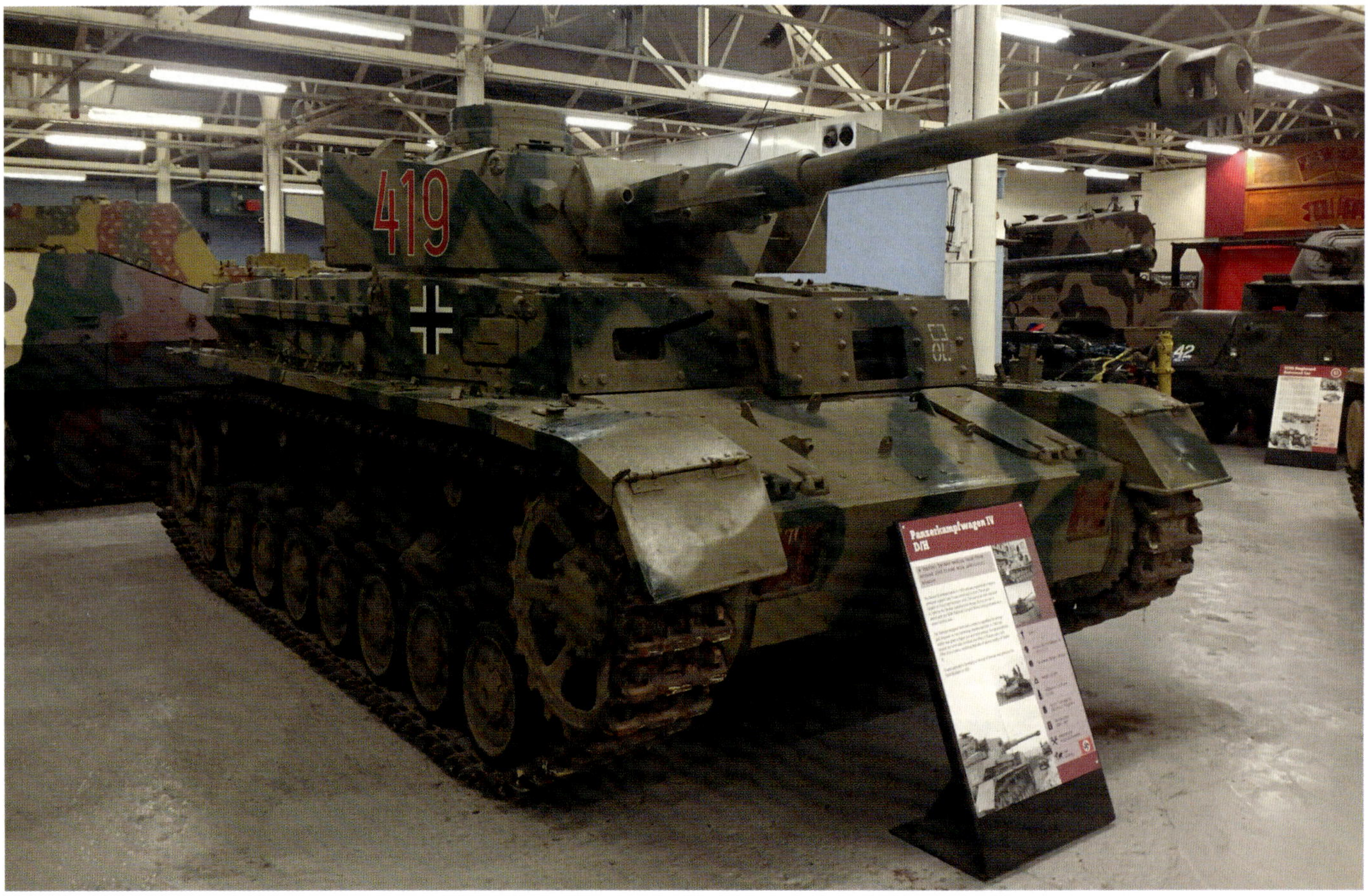

The battalion also has reconnaissance and security troops.

American infantry occupied hills on both sides of the highway. An artillery battalion sat atop a hill directly north of the road and the tank destroyers were spread out on low hills in front of the artillery. They had good observation of the road. South of the road behind the American-occupied hill sat the Chott El Guettar, a salt march impassable to vehicles.

The action began at 0445 when a German motorcyclist ran into the 601st's outpost line and was captured. He admitted 10th Panzer was attacking at 0500. Baker reported this information to his superiors and prepared his men for battle. Minutes later the men in the outposts heard the sound of armoured vehicles approaching. Soon they counted 16 enemy tanks with hundreds of infantry.

The tank destroyer crews waited until the enemy was only 200m away and opened fire. The outposts used their machine guns on the infantry. The German tanks replied, using

machine guns with tracers in the early morning dimness. When a tracer hit a tank destroyer, the tracers would ricochet upward, revealing its position for a follow up shot from the tank's cannon. Two M3s were disabled, forcing two US platoons to fall back.

The Germans split their forces, with the main group continuing down the road toward El Guettar while a second group turned to engage B and C Companies of the 601st in the hills. The M3s stayed hidden while forward observers watched the enemy and relayed their location. When an enemy tank was exposed, an M3 would quickly pull forward to a firing position, shoot, and then pull back to reload before choosing a new firing position.

A deadly game of cat and mouse ensued as German tanks sought out American tank destroyers. German infantry infiltrated into the hills while German artillery rained down. Between all the movement and firing, the morning became a swirling melee held in clouds of dust. Cannon ➤

ABOVE: An M3 tank destroyer of US II Corps on Tunisia a month after the battle. The M3 would be retired after the African campaign in favour of the turreted M10. (US ARMY)

LEFT: M10 tank destroyers of the 899th Tanks destroyer battalion were present at El Guettar but played little role in the battle. It was a more capable vehicle with a 76mm cannon in a turret and better (but still thin) armour. (US ARMY)

LEFT: General Patton was present at El Guettar. He moved around the battlefield in this specially modified scout car. (US ARMY)

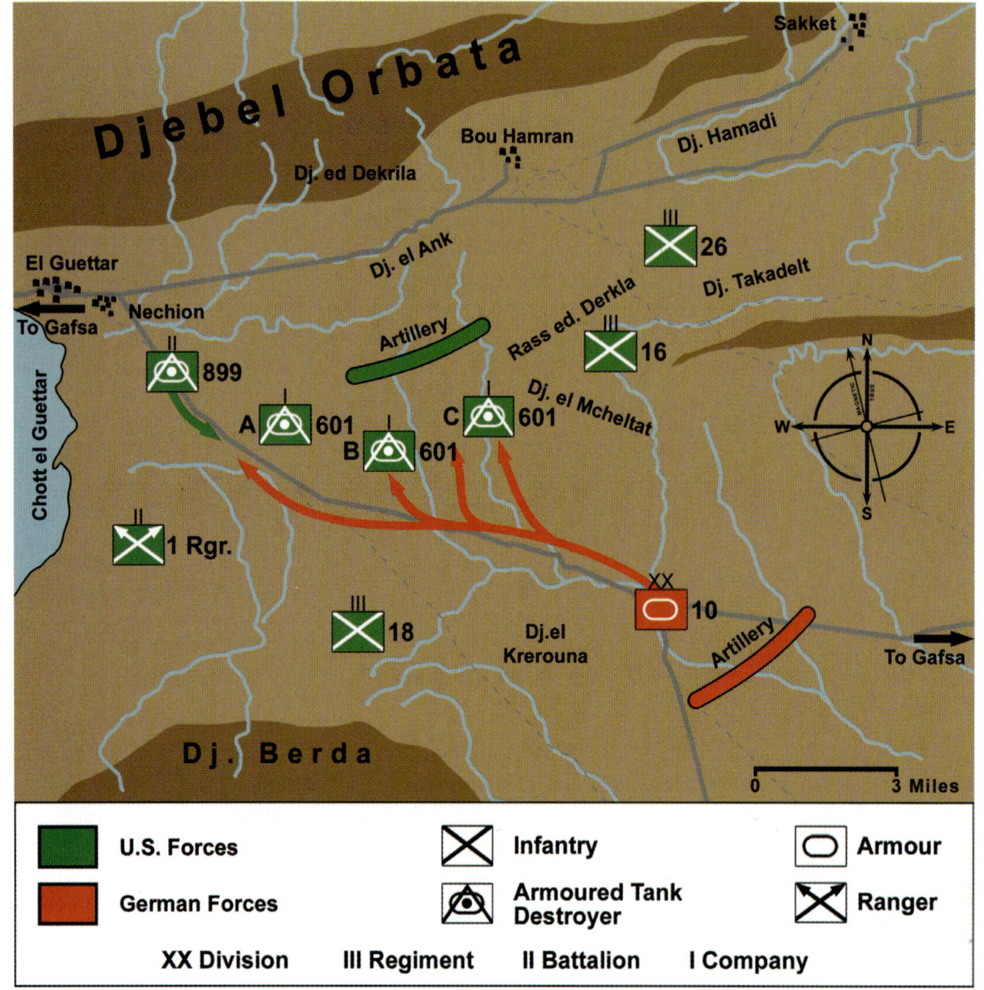

caught fire immediately. His halftrack was destroyed before he could fire another round."

That crew bailed out, and Yowell's other M3s kept shooting. "I saw Corporal Hamel destroy a Pz IV, and Sergeant Nesmith knocked the turret off a Pz IV at about one thousand yards range. Enemy infantry came in very close and their tanks were laying smoke while they brought up line after line of tanks." Yowell counted 100 enemy tanks, a misidentification since 10th Panzer did not have that many; in the chaos of combat, such errors are common.

The rest of B and C Companies fought similarly, exchanging fire with platoon-sized groups of German tanks and keeping their infantry at bay with a combination of machine gun and cannon fire. The US artillery just behind the tank destroyers had many target that morning, but managed to fire occasional volleys at nearby Germans, forcing their infantry to spread out.

The main German force continued down Highway 15 and soon came within range of A Company. The Germans spotted them and called in an artillery smoke screen. When the smoke cleared, the German column was about 2,000m away, extreme range for the M3s. Still, Baker ordered them to fire as they were getting too close to the town.

The incoming fire caused the Germans to move farther south to get out of range of the M3s. This proved bad for the Germans, as they veered into the Chott El Guettar where several tanks became bogged down. The German column also blundered into a minefield laid in a dry patch of ground. Soon eight wrecked or burning panzers littered the area. Their momentum gone, the Germans

boomed, machine guns chattered and the wounded screamed. To keep up their fire on the Germans, tank destroyer crews often had to remain in place for longer, leaving them exposed. More M3s were hit and several burned, adding smoke to the dust.

Lt. John Yowell commanded Third Platoon, B Company of the 601st. He had to reposition his M3s to get clear fields of fire on the Germans but had brief success. "Sergeant Raymond maneuvered his gun and destroyed a Pz VI [Tiger I] with six rounds, four of which bounced off the heavy armor," he wrote. "Sergeant Raymond fired one more round, at the same range, at a following tank, Pz IV, and it

withdrew, recovering four of their tanks as they left. Baker admired the German's ability to recover disabled vehicles under fire, something the American had not yet mastered.

As the main German column retreated, several of its tanks joined the attack on B and C Companies. Lt. Yowell soon lost all but two of his M3s and low on ammunition, had to fall back as well.

On the nearby hills, the infantry watched the 601st fight for its life. One witness, Capt. Sam Carter, wrote, "There were red, white and blue tracers being fired … Soon these colors were joined by green, purple, yellow and orange tracers. Soon after this the larger guns began firing. It appeared that every time there were point ricochets these would be followed by the large caliber guns. It was very dark at this time and nothing could be seen except the source of this large volume of fire slowly moving westwards... daylight started breaking and before us in the valley was an entire panzer division."

As the battle progressed, Carter saw, "Soon the valley was just a mass of guns shooting, shells bursting, armored vehicles burning and tanks moving steadily westward." Finally, at about noon the Germans withdrew, some of them taking up defensive positions just out of range of the tank destroyers. Carter watched the Germans recovered some disabled tanks. "This was done in the midst of artillery fire which did not seem to faze those working outside the tanks at all."

Around noon, an American halftrack towing a cannon appeared. The 601st's men held their fire

thinking it was a stray US unit. Suddenly the halftrack stopped and seven Germans jumped out and started setting up the gun. An M3 crews quickly fired three explosive rounds, destroying the vehicle and killing five of the Germans. The remaining two were soon captured.

After a brief air raid, a second German attack began in late afternoon. Two battalions of Panzer Grenadiers advanced ahead of the remaining panzers. When they were 1,500m away US artillery opened fire, pummelling them with high explosive rounds set with timed fuses so they exploded just above the ground.

The 601st joined in firing at the enemy tanks and infantry with cannon and machine guns. Baker

watched as a sergeant "bracketed rapidly and fired as fast as he could, making 5-mil deflection changes. He dropped high-explosive shells at 7-yard intervals across the German lines." This broke the German attack and ended the Battle of El Guettar.

The battle took a heavy toll; the 601st lost 21 of 31 M3s and fired 2,740 rounds of 75mm ammunition; its standard load was 2,844. The 601st also fired 50,000 rounds of small arms ammunition. They received credit for 30 of the 37 panzers knocked out that day and 200 enemy infantry. The Americans were battered, but not broken. They took the German's best shot at El Guettar and did not give way, teaching a lesson of their own that day.

Kursk

The cauldron of German defeat

Nazi Germany lost the initiative by mid-1943. The Western Allies liberated North Africa and were in Italy, with the promise of the D-Day landings looming. On the Eastern Front, the long-beleaguered Soviets defeated the Nazi war machine at Stalingrad and were now ready for further offensive action.

However, the Germans were not out of the fight. They still retained most of their conquered territory and impressive combat power. The spring thaw, beginning in March 1943, forced an operational pause to both sides, allowing them to rebuild and prepare for renewed fighting. The German realised they were incapable of a major summer offensive as they had been in 1941 and 1942. Instead, they hoped smaller but bold attacks could keep the Soviets off balance and unable to launch a major offensive, allowing Germany more time to recover.

The area around Kursk held a Russian salient, a bulge in the front line extending deep into German-held territory. The German high command developed a plan called *Zitadelle* (Citadel), aiming large forces at the flanks of the salient in a pincer attack. Success would cut off the forces in the salient, enabling their destruction; it would also shorten the front line, allowing the Germans to defend it with less troops.

The Germans committed most of their available armour in the east to this operation. This included not only Tiger tanks but also the then-new Panther tank and Ferdinand tank destroyer. Some planners thought these new weapons would turn the balance back in their favour, but others thought the plan seriously flawed. The salient was an obvious place for an attack and the Soviets would be ready. The plan assumed German success despite Soviet defences and improvements. Unknown to them, the Soviet spy network in Germany knew about Citadel and passed the information along to the Soviet command.

Knowing where the attack was coming allowed the Soviets to prepare extensive defences. They constructed three defensive belts to a depth of 40km. Each kilometre of the front held 1,400 anti-tank mines. The Soviets massed 20,000 cannon, one-third of them anti-tank guns, along with 3,300 tanks to support the 1.5 million troops emplaced for the battle. The Germans employed about 800,000 soldiers with 3,000 tanks.

Originally scheduled for 5 May, Hitler postponed the operation several times to wait for enough of the new tanks to reach the front. Finally, the operation began on 5 July, but did not get off to a good start. The new Panthers experienced problems due to their rushed development; many of them caught fire or broke down on the way from the railheads to the combat area. In the north, the German 9th Army attacked south while the 4th Panzer Army attacked to the north, hoping to meet at Kursk in the salient's centre. Both ran into a storm of fire.

Soviet commanders dug in their anti-tank guns and some tanks, hardening them against German tank and artillery fire. Other tank units were kept in reserve to attack into the German flanks once their forces were committed. German tank crews relied on the high quality of their vehicles, combat experience and their high standards of training to deal with such attacks.

The Battle of Kursk saw massive numbers of troops, tanks, artillery and aircraft employed in combined arms combat over a vast area. Rather than attempt to encapsulate the entire battle into a few pages, instead we present two vignettes of significant armour actions within the larger operation.

Panthers in action for the first time

The Panther's poor performance at Kursk belied its later effectiveness once the design matured. The 39th Panzer Regiment, one of the first units to be equipped with the Panther, boasted 200 of them on 4 July 1943. By 6 July only 40 Panthers remained operational. Some succumbed to enemy fire or mines but the majority simply broke down.

On 6 July, the operational Panthers went forward in an attack against prepared Soviet positions near the village of Alekseyevka. Three companies of dug-in T-34s of the 14th Tank Regiment reinforced infantry and anti-tank guns, entrenched behind an anti-tank ditch and a minefield. More T-34s ➤

LEFT: Soviet infantry follow KV and T-34 tanks at Kursk on 12 July. Armed with submachine guns, they could lay down heavy fire on German anti-tank emplacements within their limited range. (RUSSIAN MOD)

BELOW: Though this image is from three months before Kursk, it shows the Soviet 45mm anti-tank gun in action. By mid-1943 it was largely ineffective against German tanks but could still knock out lighter armoured vehicles. (POLISH ARCHIVES)

BOTTOM: A Panther and Panzer III pause during the Kursk fighting. The Panther in the background has been disabled by a mine. (US NATIONAL ARCHIVES)

RIGHT: By mid-1943 Panzer IVs were fitted with armoured skirts on their hulls and turrets, so they were often misidentified as Tigers, especially at long range. (US NATIONAL ARCHIVES)

stood ready to support and the whole position was formed in what is known as an L-shaped ambush, where the enemy runs into the short leg of the L to its front so the troops in the long leg of the L can fire into the enemy's flank.

After a delay when the lead Panther unit became lost, they ran into a minefield. This immobilised some Panthers and the unit stopped. Soviet artillery quickly rained down on them and the dug-in T-34s opened fire at a range of 1,000-1,200m. Against the Panther's frontal armour the range would have been too long, but the Soviets were able to hit the Panthers in their thinner flank armour. The heavy Soviet fire soon knocked out several Panthers, including at least one hit in the fuel cell, setting it alight.

The German's opened fire on the T-34s, difficult shots since only the turrets of the Soviet tanks were exposed when they popped up to fire. Still, the better German gunnery training enabled their gunners to hit several T-34s, causing many of the rest to reposition. This allowed the rest of the German tanks to withdraw and get out of the ambush kill zone. They soon crossed the anti-tank ditch and laagered for the night, having lost 19 Panthers.

The next day the German managed to get 50 Panthers operational and sent them to seize the town of Dubrova and then move against the Soviets at Syrtsev. Again, the Soviets placed entrenched T-34s and a few 85mm anti-tank guns near the town. As the day before, they waited until the advancing Germans hit a minefield before opening fire, again hitting them in their side armour. Soon another 15 Panthers were lost. Soviet Lt. Vasily Bryukhov recalled, "I'd get a target in the gun sight – a short stop, one shot, another one. I'd traverse the gun from left to right...Only when the tank was hit by an armour-piercing round...

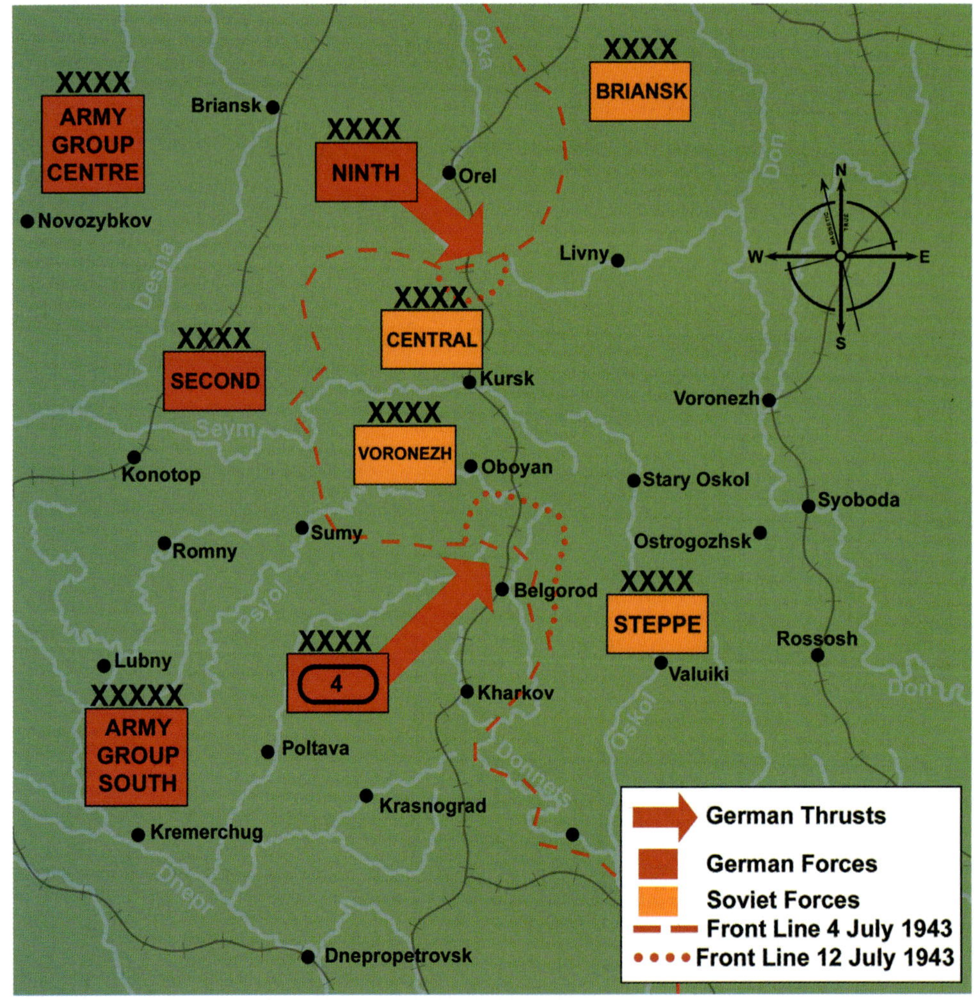

would I realise that there were also some guys firing at me."

The German used their accurate 75mm guns to destroy many Soviet tanks and then supported the infantry as they assaulted the enemy positions. By dusk they had overrun the Soviets but only 20 Panthers remained operational. For a long time afterward, the Germans referred to the fighting as 'the Panther cemetery at Dubrova.'

Prokhorovka

One of history's largest tank battles, on 12 July the Germans II SS Panzer Corps advanced toward the town, deep in the Soviet's third defensive belt, at about 08:00 AM. They had about 300 tanks and assault guns, including 15 Tiger Is. As they moved, hundreds of Soviet T-34s appeared ahead of them, moving fast. The Soviets had about 800 tanks and self-propelled guns available, and 500 of them from the 5th Guards Tank Army (5GTA) now bore down on the Germans.

The Soviets recognised the German advantage in long range gunnery, so they planned to use the T-34's mobility to close the distance and negate the German advantages in firepower and armour protection. According to the Russian history of the battle, the tank charge also "destroyed the enemy's ability to control his leading unit and subunits." At close range the panzer's advantages diminished. "There were frequent explosions as ammunition blew up, throwing tank turrets dozens of yards… smashed tanks were blazing like torches. It was difficult to tell who was attacking and who was defending. The fortunes of the combatants varied from place to place."

Georg Lötzsch commanded a Tiger I during the battle. His tank, with three other Tigers, sat on high ground when a mass of 50 Soviet tanks in wedge formation attacked them. The Germans poured fire into the wedge, destroying many T-34s before having to move to engage another Soviet unit. One Tiger was immobilised and had to be abandoned.

There is considerable argument over how many tanks were destroyed at Prokhorovka; the original numbers ran into the many hundreds on each side. A more recent estimate places the count at about 540 Soviet armoured vehicles, of which over 200 were repairable. German loss estimates range from an absurdly low three up to around 80, many of which were also likely repairable.

Whatever the numbers, the battle prevented the Germans from creating a breach in the Soviet lines and the battle soon ended when German forces became exhausted. Today Prokhorovka is considered one of Russia's most important battles, similar to Waterloo in the UK or Gettysburg in the US.

ABOVE: A Tiger moving on the north side of the Kursk salient. Relatively few Tigers were present at the battle but made a significant impact. Within a year new weapons would make the Tiger I less of a threat. (US NATIONAL ARCHIVES)

BELOW: A view of the Kursk battlefield from a Panzer III turret. The Panzer IV in the background has lost one of its armoured skirts; this happened frequently in action. (US NATIONAL ARCHIVES)

Panzer IVs and T-34s

Many accounts of German armour tend to focus on the formidable Tigers and Panthers, but the Panzer IV was Germany's most numerous tank, with almost 8,300 produced, not including chassis produced as assault guns and other variants. Compared to its larger brethren, the medium Panzer IV was nimble and reliable; by mid-war, its short-barrelled 75mm gun was replaced by a long-barrelled high-velocity 75mm cannon, the KwK 40 L/48, which had good armour penetration out to 1,500m against comparable Allied tanks like the Sherman and T-34.

Bruno Friesen served as a gunner on a Panzer IV in 1944. Born in Canada to German-Ukrainian Mennonite immigrants, Bruno's parents made the fateful decision to move to Germany in the 1930s. At the time, Germany must have seemed on the rise to Bruno's culturally German family, who sought better opportunities. Instead, Bruno and his younger brother Oscar were soon in the Wehrmacht, with a Bruno a tank crewman. His brother died near Houffalize, Belgium in 1944, killed by a strafing Allied aircraft.

By 1944 Bruno served in the 8th Company, Panzer Regiment 25 of the 7th Panzer Division. On route to this new assignment, he and 84 other newly trained tank crewmen took possession of 17 new Panzer IVs at the factory. With the tanks loaded onto a train, they travelled east and joined their unit at Chernovtsy, then part of

LEFT: The T-34/85 made its combat debut during the winter of 1944. Its 85mm gun, adapted from an anti-aircraft weapon, gave it better odds against German panzers. (US NATIONAL ARCHIVES)

Romania, now part of Ukraine, in late March 1944. The Soviets captured the city a week later. His war as a tank gunner was about to begin.

A few days later, Bruno's company sat in a wooded area, overlooking a main road. They had used a small forestry service road to find a position where they could ambush any advancing Soviet units. April is a wet month in the region; fields are sodden and ditches full of water. Tanks which tried to cross either risked becoming mired. Vehicles of either army stuck to the roads. The Germans camouflaged their vehicles with local foliage and branches.

The Panzer IV's armour is mainly vertical, with no slope to decrease the chance of penetration by an enemy armour-piercing (AP) shell. To improve their protection., the tank crews parked their panzers at an angle, with either front corner of the vehicle facing the road. This put the frontal armour at an angle against incoming fire. While this gave better chances for the tank as a whole, the driver and radio operator, who sat in the tank's hull, were at a disadvantage. Depending in which corner was presented to the enemy, the tank's main gun barrel would be over their hatch. When a Panzer IV had a full load of 87 rounds of ammunition, as these did, those crewmen could not escape by climbing into the turret. Thus, they could be trapped in the hull. A risk likely never envisaged by the Panzer IV's designers, but one which the crew had to bear.

Very soon, enemy tanks appeared. Single file on the road, 19 T-34/85s appeared, each tank carrying a group of infantry on its back; Bruno referred to them as 'swarms of bees.' Carrying a powerful 85mm gun in an enlarged turret, the improved T-34/85 model had only recently entered Soviet service. The German 75mm cannon held armour-piercing rounds, each meant for an enemy tank. With the gunner's focus on the tanks, he would be unable to use the coaxial machine gun, so the radio operator would use the hull machine gun against the infantry, who would jump from the T-34s when the firing began.

At 250m, the Germans opened fire. Bruno hit his target, watching ⬤

BELOW: A group of *tankodesantniki*, or 'tank riders,' leap from a T-34. When the tank came under fire, they had to immediately disembark, or risk being hit. They protected the tank from close infantry attack. (RUSSIAN ARCHIVES – PUBLIC DOMAIN)

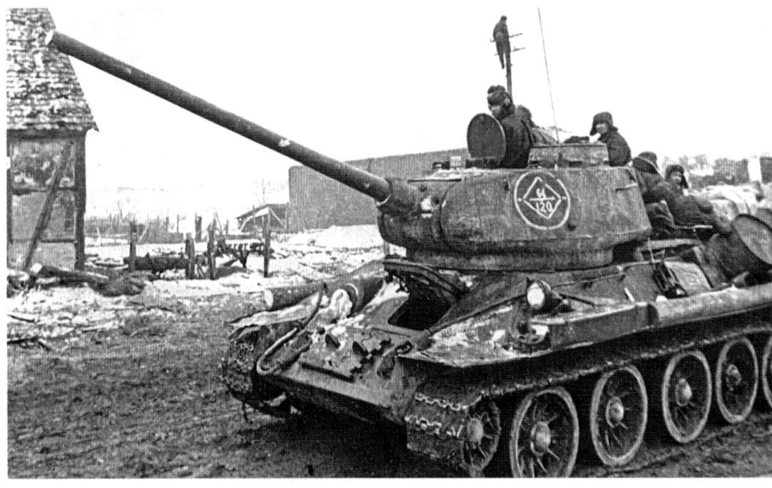

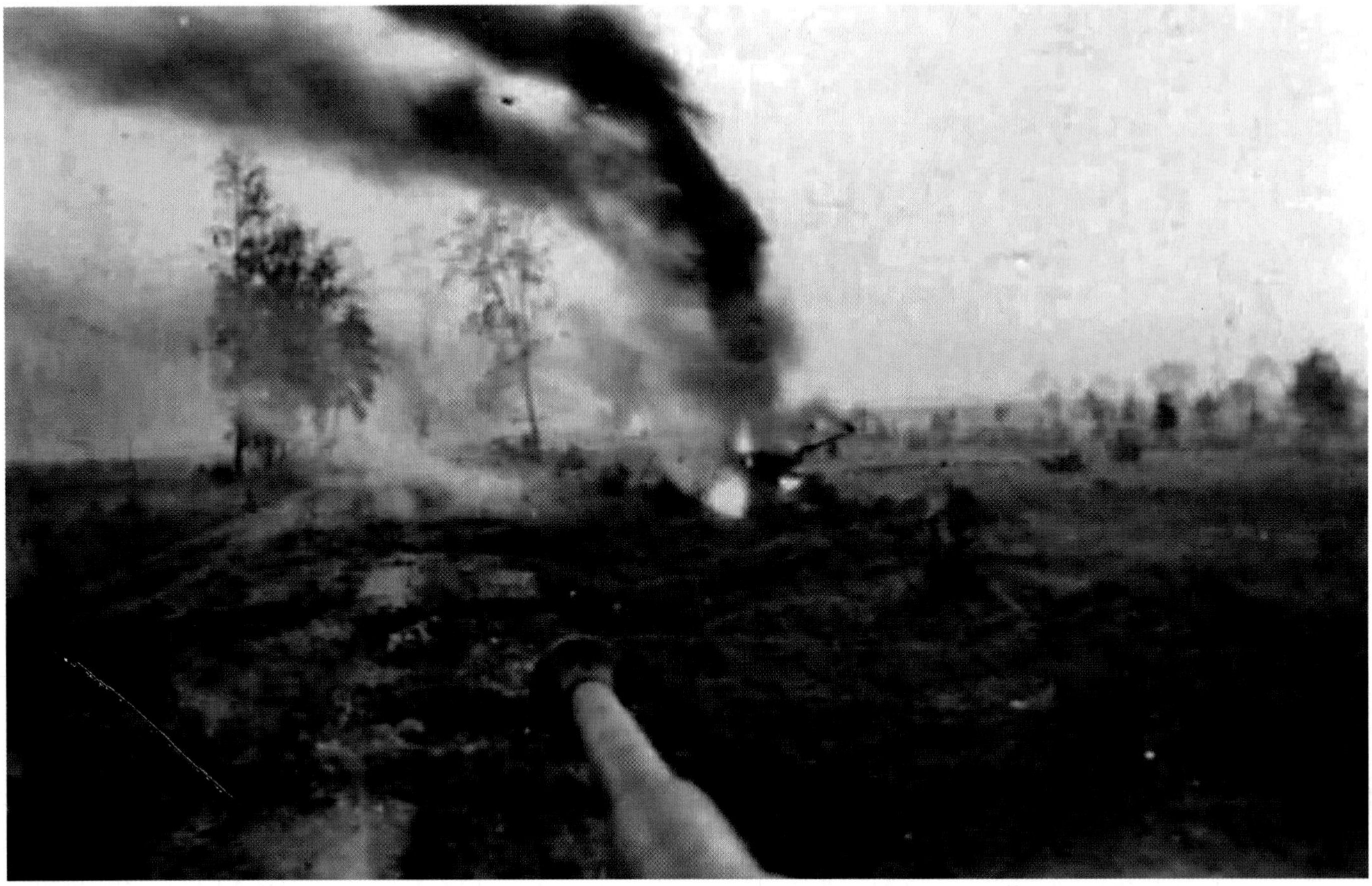

ABOVE: A T-34 burns ahead of a German tank, likely a Tiger I. The wet conditions at certain times of year created deep mud, forcing many battles to occur around roads. (BUNDESARCHIV)

the enemy infantry leap from the now-doomed Soviet tank, which soon burst into flame. The other German tanks scored hits as well; the area right around the road became a charnel house, obscured by the smoke of burning tanks and the cries of wounded soldiers. Some of the T-34s returned fire, knocking out two Panzer IVs before the Soviet unit fought through the ambush and continued down the road southward. They left at least eight wrecked T-34s by Bruno's count, the hulks sitting on or around the road. The action lasted perhaps ten minutes.

The company commander quickly checked his unit. The crews of the two destroyed panzers were alive, salvaging what they could from their immobilised machines. They would either ride on another tank or move on foot to the rear to rejoin the regiment. It appeared the surviving Soviet infantry managed to climb aboard the remaining T-34s when they moved south. The rest of the company waited for orders.

The German commander decided to leave the bulk of company in place and take three panzers to pursue the Soviet force on the road. The tanks remaining in position would engage any other Soviets appearing on the road. The T-34 and Panzer IV had about the same top speed, but the Soviets would have to go slower to watch out for mines or other ambushes. All tankers feared mines, particularly the hapless driver and radio operator in the hull. A mine explosion almost always caused them injury and would disable their tank.

The order came, "Pursue immediately!" Bruno's tank and two others left the woods and moved onto the main road, moving south after their prey. Well-stocked with ammunition and fuel, the trio of panzers accelerated to their top speed of 48km/h. If they moved fast the Soviets would not have time to lay any mines of their own. The worst danger came from a Soviet rear guard laying an ambush of its own.

The German tanks sped on, no flank ambush appearing. They searched for the Soviet column, knowing their 75mm guns could easily tear through the thin rear armour of a T-34. Bruno knew an AP round from his cannon might go entirely through the T-34's 45mm rear hull armour, through the engine compartment and into the crew area. His other option involved aiming just above the hull at the turret rear. A round there would strike the turret's rear overhang, either penetrating the turret itself or ricocheting down into the turret ring, disabling it.

After a chase of 5km, the panzers caught up with the Soviet column just around a bend in the road, with the T-34s spaced out unevenly over several hundred metres. They seemed unaware of their German pursuers, having posted no rear guard. The Soviets would pay dearly for that error.

RIGHT: The T-34/85 also introduced a larger turret with room for a gunner, loader and commander. This allowed the leader to focus on commanding the tank and provided enough crew to run the main gun. (US NATIONAL ARCHIVES)

LEFT: Later in the war, many Panzer IVs were fitted with *schürzen*, thin metal plates which gave stand-off protection against some anti-tank weapons. The hull plates were often torn off during operations as the tank struck objects or moved in rough terrain. (US NATIONAL ARCHIVES)

The Germans planned to fire two volleys and then try to knock out the lead T-34, trapping the remaining enemy tanks on the road to be destroyed. Soviet tanks could pivot in place to bring their armament and thicker frontal armour to bear, so the plan was risky, but presented their best chance to eliminate two companies of Soviet tanks. At 300m, Bruno and his comrades stopped to increase their accuracy and opened fire.

The first volleys from the panzers left four T-34s burning. The remaining seven kept moving but traversed their turrets to the rear to engage as they kept moving southward. Bruno later wrote of the scene, "Parthian archers in 1944 Romania." The Panzer IVs remained still, firing at the T-34s as the Soviet gunners fired back from the move, now 500m away. Bruno's loader slammed AP rounds into the breech of the 75mm gun as fast as he could, the young gunner aiming at his moving targets, calculating the required lead using the formula taught to him during his panzer gunner's training just a few months earlier.

Another T-34 in the enemy column burst into flame and veered off the western edge of the road. Then, with the enemy column 650m away, a Soviet shell struck Bruno's tank. It failed to penetrate the tank's armour but instead glanced along the turret where it met the top of the tank's hull. This left a 20cm-long gouge in the tank's armour – Bruno described it as "a kind of gigantic spot-weld" – that froze the turret in place so it could no longer traverse.

The remaining six T-34s disappeared into the distance while the three panzers returned to the rest of the 8th Company. Bruno's damaged tank took the centre position in the formation, with one panzer ahead and the other behind, the rear tank's turret traversed to guard their withdrawal. They returned without incident, but the smoke of the burning T-34s on the road alerted a Soviet follow-on force that there had been a battle. Deducing the German's likely location, the Soviets unleashed a 120mm mortar barrage that lasted 30 minutes.

The company commander decided to go over to the attack, rather than wait for more Soviets. He ordered Bruno's crews to blow up their tank and escape on foot after the rest of the company moved out. This would distract the Soviets and give them a chance to escape. The crew took one of their MG-34 machine guns and several belts of ammunition before Bruno set the fuse on the tank's demolition charge. Ninety seconds later, the turret flew from the hull in a large explosion.

The crew made their way back to German lines and later rejoined the unit in time to see action in Lithuania in July 1944. Bruno survived the war and later returned to Canada, married, and eventually became a professor of English.

BELOW: Later in the war Bruno Friesen became a crewmember in a Jagdpanzer IV/70 tank destroyer. It carried a high velocity 75mm cannon and thick frontal armour. (US NATIONAL ARCHIVES)

Operation Goodwood

The British Army's largest tank battle in Europe

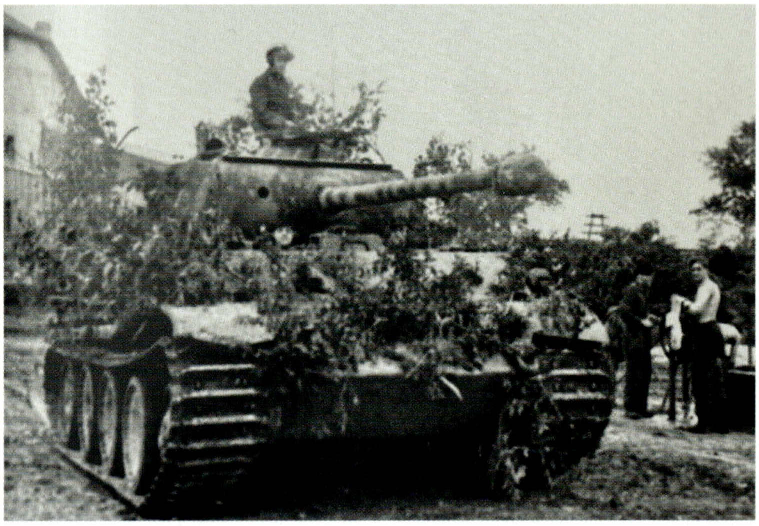

RIGHT: A camouflaged Panther tank in France. Only a few dozen were available during Operation Goodwood, but its 75mm gun was deadly to Shermans and Cromwells. (BUNDESARCHIV BILD 101L-301-1955-32-KURTH-CC-BY-SA 3.0)

After capturing the northern part of Caen, British Gen. Montgomery planned a new offensive, aimed at capturing the southern part of Caen and the Bourguebus Ridge south of the city. Seizing this area provided several advantages, chiefly the ability to break out into better terrain for armoured operations and to pin down German armour. This would prevent the German tanks from shifting south to resist the upcoming US Operation Cobra, designed to break American forces out of the easily defensible bocage country.

This plan, Operation Goodwood, used three armoured divisions, the Guards, 11th and 7th, formed into the VIII Corps under Gen. O'Connor, of North Africa fame. Montgomery selected armoured units largely because the British Army had suffered heavy casualties in their infantry units during the prior fighting in Normandy and were low on replacements. Thanks to Allied industrial production, Montgomery could afford to replace tanks more easily than infantry.

Canals and the Orne River ran north past Caen to the sea. VIII Corps moved across these and into position north of their objectives. When the operation began, British I Corps would attack to protect VIII Corps left flank while Canadian II Corps would strike south from Caen on their right. The Guards and 11th Armoured Divisions primarily used the Sherman while Cromwells equipped the 7th Armoured. All three divisions had Sherman Firefly tanks with their powerful 17-pounder anti-tank guns, usually issued at one Firefly in each four-tank troop. British tank strength stood at 1,163 tanks at the beginning of the operation.

German strength stood much lower at about 150 tanks, mainly from the 21st Panzer and 1st SS Panzer Divisions, but also Heavy Panzer Battalion 503, equipped with Tigers. The Germans also possessed assault guns, self-propelled tank destroyers and many anti-tank guns, including the powerful 88mm PaK 43. Some of the German armoured vehicles were rebuilt conversions of French vehicles captured in 1940.

The ground for the operation appeared to be good tank country and mostly was, except for several railroad embankments and a few large hedgerows which would hinder the British advance. Another problem lay in the bridgehead on the east side of the Orne River; it was so narrow the

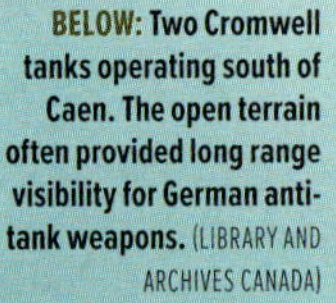

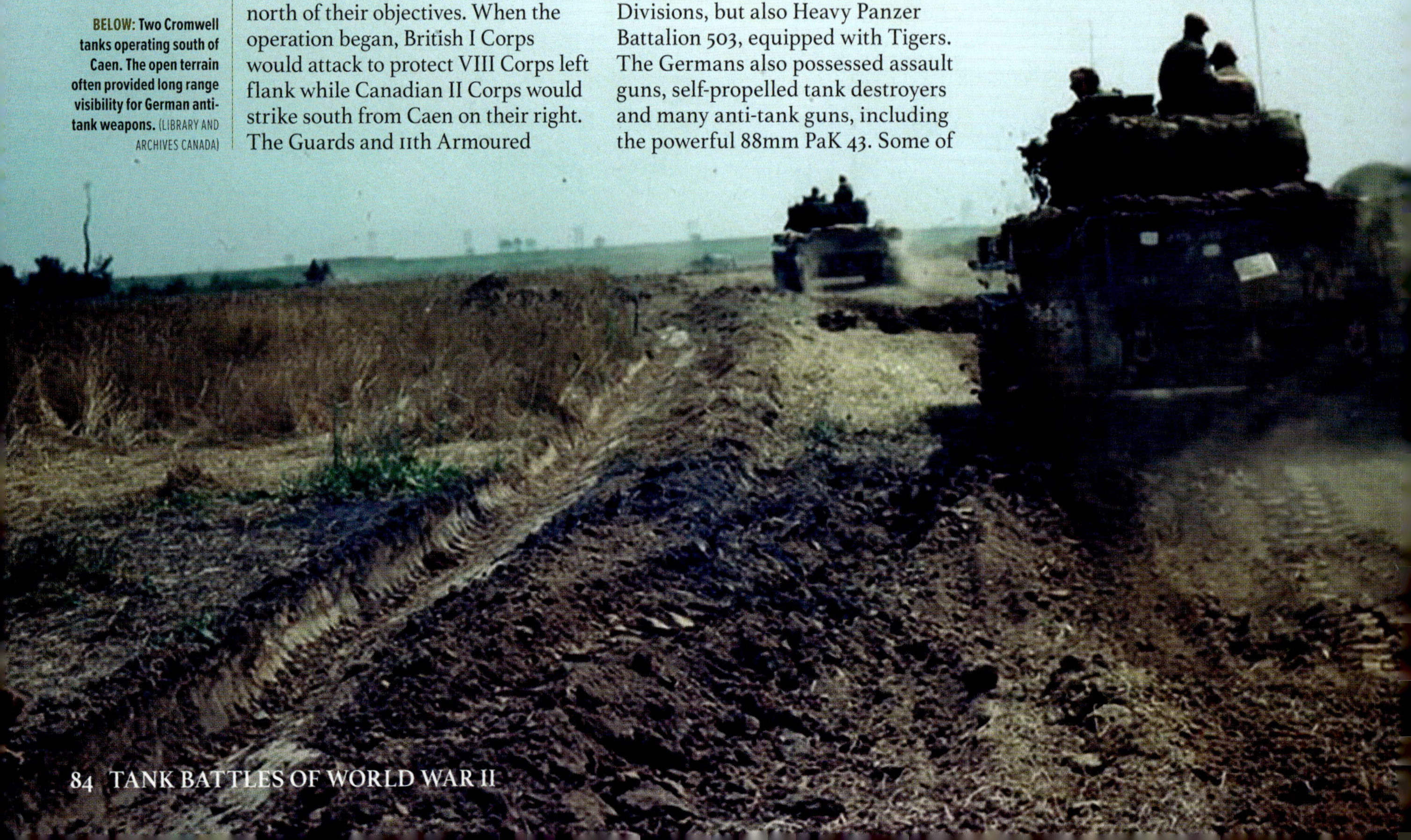

BELOW: Two Cromwell tanks operating south of Caen. The open terrain often provided long range visibility for German anti-tank weapons. (LIBRARY AND ARCHIVES CANADA)

three British armoured division could only attack in column, one behind the other. The Germans defences consisted of four defensive belts up to 16km deep in places. Critically, these included villages fortified with anti-tank guns and artillery as well as several pieces of high ground the German controlled. From this high ground they saw the British forces assembling and so knew an attack was coming.

The battle began on 18 July with a sequence of massive airstrikes using some 1,850 heavy and medium bombers, British and American. Arriving in three waves between 05:30 and 09:30 AM, the bombing was not always accurate but succeeded in smashing the forward German defences. British artillery began a creeping barrage at 0745 with the 11th following close behind. For the first several hours the advance went well. The German troops, stunned by the airstrikes, put up little resistance.

By late morning, however, the Germans began to recover, remanning their anti-tank guns and armour. Armour-piercing shot tore into the British formations as they continued forward, hoping to seize as much ground as possible before the Germans reconstituted their lines. Tragically, the battle devolved into a killing field where the Germans held a strong defensive advantage. Their 75 and 88mm guns had no problem punching through the armour of the Shermans and Cromwells, which were crowded into a narrow front, giving their enemy numerous targets.

In some places British tank crews survived by hiding their tank among the destroyed hulks. Some German gunners became confused by so many tanks in front of them that, amid the smoke and flames, they could not tell which tanks were destroyed and so put multiple rounds into abandoned vehicles.

Still, not everything went well for the Germans. They lost tanks of their own, including several to friendly fire. Lost panzers could not easily be replaced, so German crews made great efforts to recover lost tanks, especially after dark. Demolished anti-tank guns littered the field and many of the Germans dazed by the various bombardments were marched off as prisoners.

After the maelstrom of the first day, further British attacks managed to secure several more villages and strongpoints. By 20 July the British focused on consolidating their gains while the German made several counterattacks, all of which failed. By 21 July, both sides reached exhaustion and the fighting ended. What follows are vignettes highlighting the heavy fighting.

The Advance

The initial British advance benefitted from the bombing. Sgt. 'Buck' Kite of 3RTR recalled "found myself looking down the barrel of an SP gun with the crew milling around it but they were so bomb happy they didn't know what day it was."

As the Germans recovered, however, they placed a murderous fire on the ❯

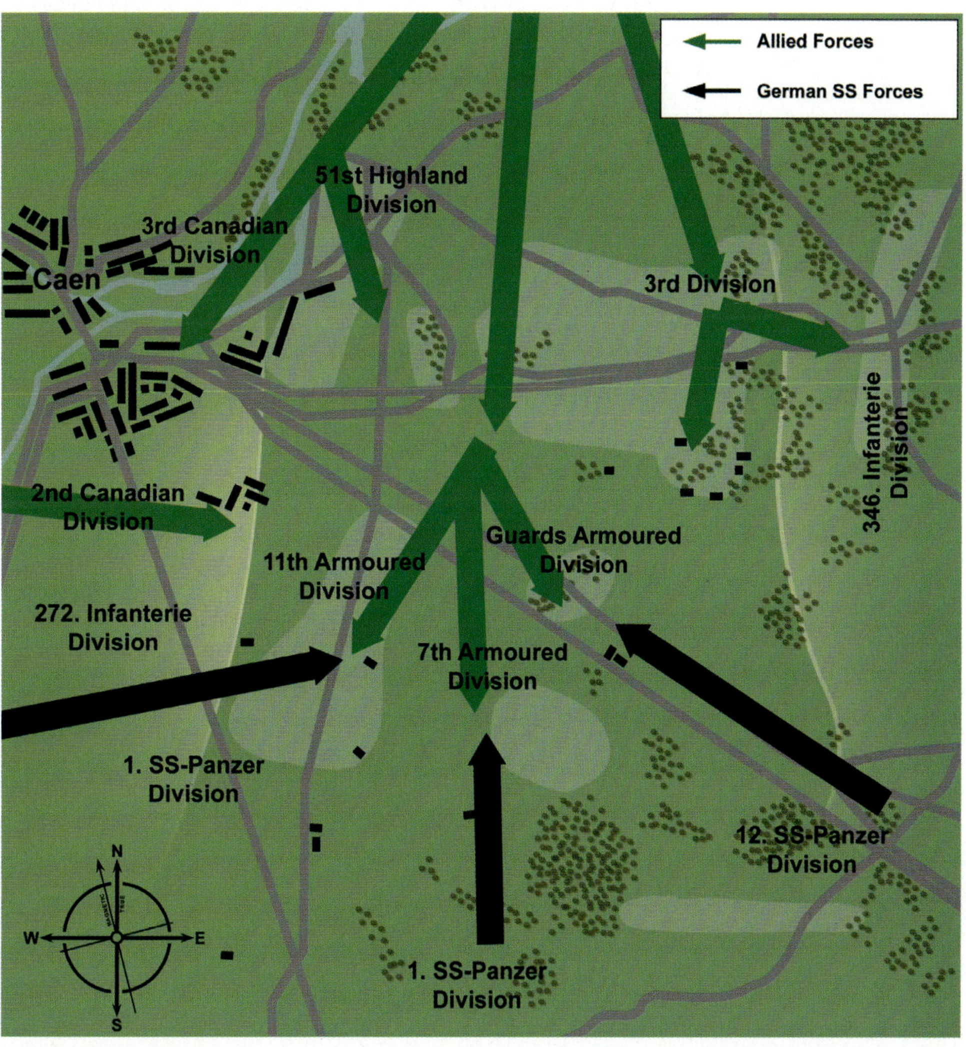

British. Lt. Steel Brownlie of the 11th Division's Fife and Forfar Yeomanry recalled being fired at by a self-propelled gun, "and two tanks to the right of me went up in smoke. To the southeast was an artillery position… I did an HE shoot on them, until they shut up…" A Panther tank appeared next. "My Charlie tank brewed it with its 17-pounder," Brownlie recalled.

Losses mounted, with a Coldstream Guardsman noting "the horizon was covered with burning Shermans. I could count nearly twenty, a whole Squadron, burning in one field alone." Still, the British tank crews hit back when they could. One officer saw a Nebelwerfer rocket launcher, dreaded by Allied troops, about to fire. He stated, "…before the last of its six barrels had been emptied the turrets of a dozen Shermans swung round and blew it and the crew to pieces – the best thing we had ever seen happen to this diabolical weapon."

RIGHT: A Panzer IV moves through a French village. The muzzles cover on the main gun and the lack of helmets on the infantry indicate they are likely out of the battle area. (BUNDESARCHIV BILD 101I-297-1722-29)

RIGHT: A Tiger I in France. Though still a formidable tank, by mid-1944 it was losing it edge over Allied tanks. Several were lost during Operation Goodwood, mostly to the bombing strikes. (BUNDESARCHIV)

Tigers in action

The new Tiger II tank first saw combat during Operation Goodwood. Tiger Is were also present, though a number were destroyed or damaged by the air bombardment. At noon on 18 July a company of Tiger IIs emerged from the hedgerows of a horse farm to attack west into British lines.

The Tiger II's first combat appearance proved inauspicious. The company commander's tank became

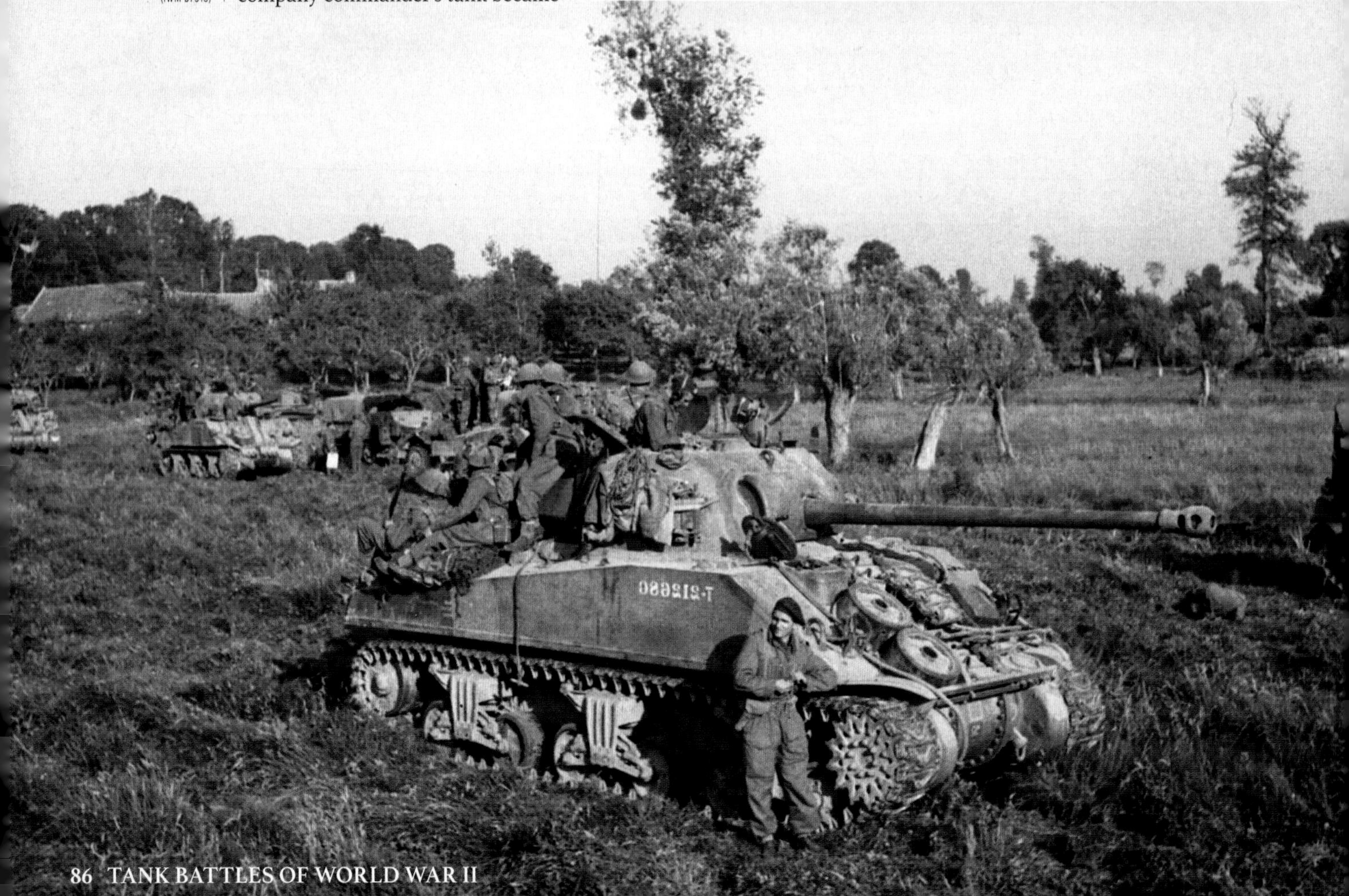

BELOW: A unit of Sherman tanks awaits orders to move out at the beginning of Operation Goodwood. Note the infantry sitting atop the Sherman Firefly. (IWM B7513)

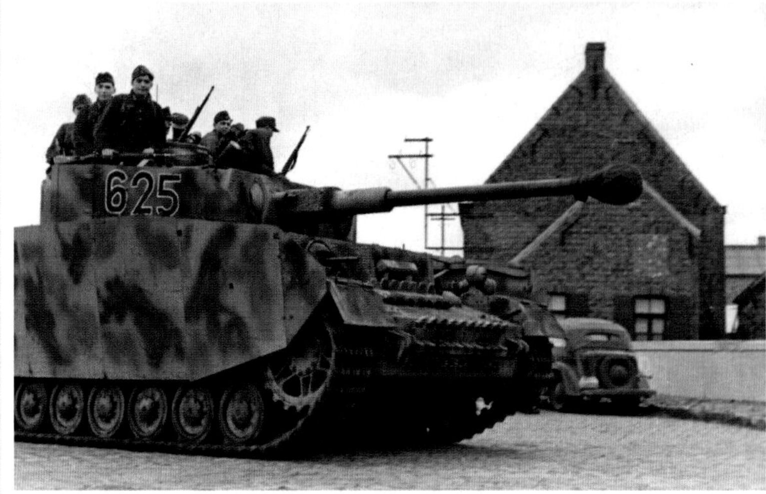

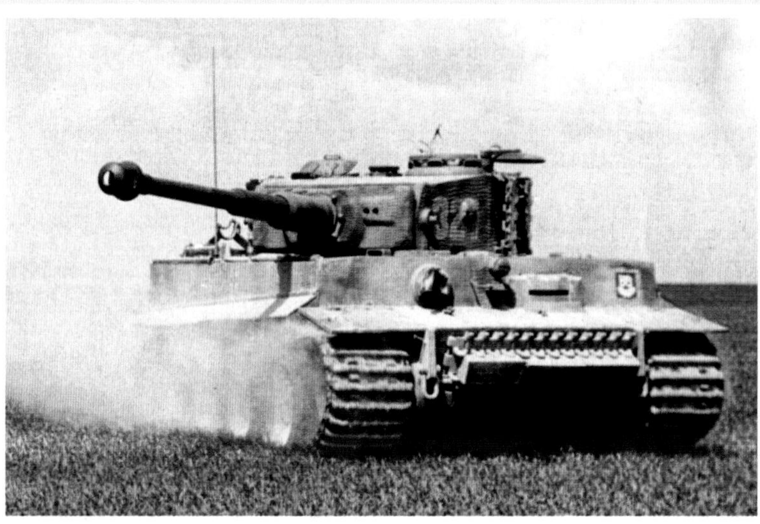

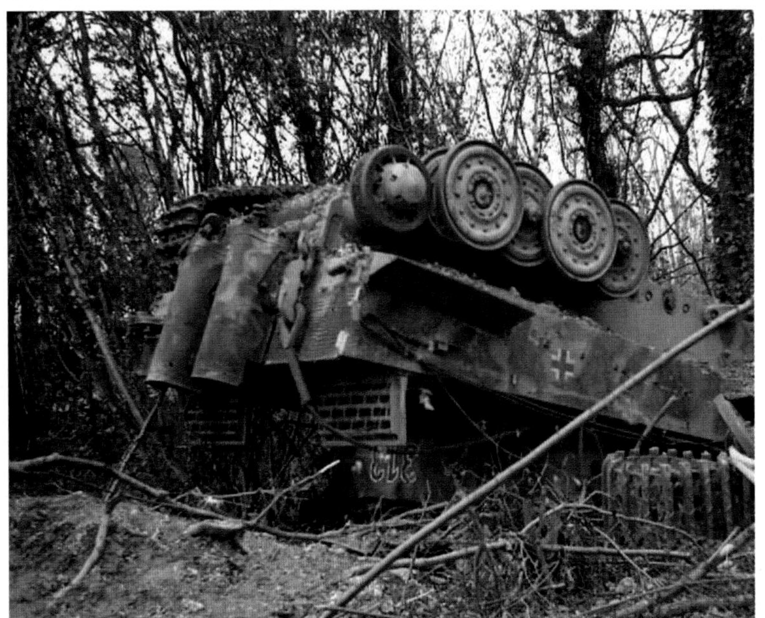

stuck in a bomb crater. A Firefly from the Coldstream Guards under Lt. Malcolm Lock is believed to have knocked out one Tiger; a second lost a few minutes later may have fallen to friendly fire. The rest of the company retreated.

Later, Lt. John Gorman of the Irish Guards, commanding a 75mm-armed Sherman named *Ballyraggett*, rounded a hedgerow to see a Tiger II about 300 yards away, under fire from several British tanks. The Tiger had become separated from its unit and was under the command of an inexperienced sergeant. Gorman ordered his gunner to fire at it, only to see the round bounce off the Tiger and into the air. Worse, the gun jammed after that shot. Gorman gave a rare order, "Driver, ram!"

The driver accelerated, ramming the 30-ton Sherman into the Tiger's left rear. Seconds later, a round penetrated the Tiger near the track. This was possibly a German anti-tank gun trying to destroy *Ballyraggett*. Both tank's crews bailed out, but neither crew were armed. After a brief argument over which crew was being taken prisoner, they each ran away in different directions.

Gorman led his crew in search of an operational tank and found a Firefly with a dead commander and the crew in shock. He assumed command and took the Sherman back to the Tiger II, destroyed it with several rounds, gathered some British wounded and evacuated them. Gorman later received a Military Cross.

Goodwood affected Heavy Panzer Battalion 503. Before this they had always been essentially invulnerable on the battlefield. Now, for the first time they felt they had failed. The battalion historian stated, "the war there forced us into another dimension that we had not yet known and in which we were inferior. We were crushed in battle by an unimaginable material superiority."

Operation Goodwood cost the British 493 tanks knocked out, though many of them proved repairable. German tank losses stood at 45-85, depending on source. The operation remains controversial; it was launched partly due to political pressure between the allies and the high losses caused recriminations and revised explanations afterward. Whatever the case, it succeeded in keeping Germany's armour away from the American breakout and inflicted losses they could not afford.

LEFT: The bombing attacks by Allied aircraft were so intense even 60-ton Tiger tanks were flipped over by the blasts. (IWM B8032)

BELOW: A Sherman moves past a destroyed Panzer IV near the French town of Cagny during Goodwood. The haze in this image shows how the dust and smoke hung over the battlefield on the first day. (IWM B7760)

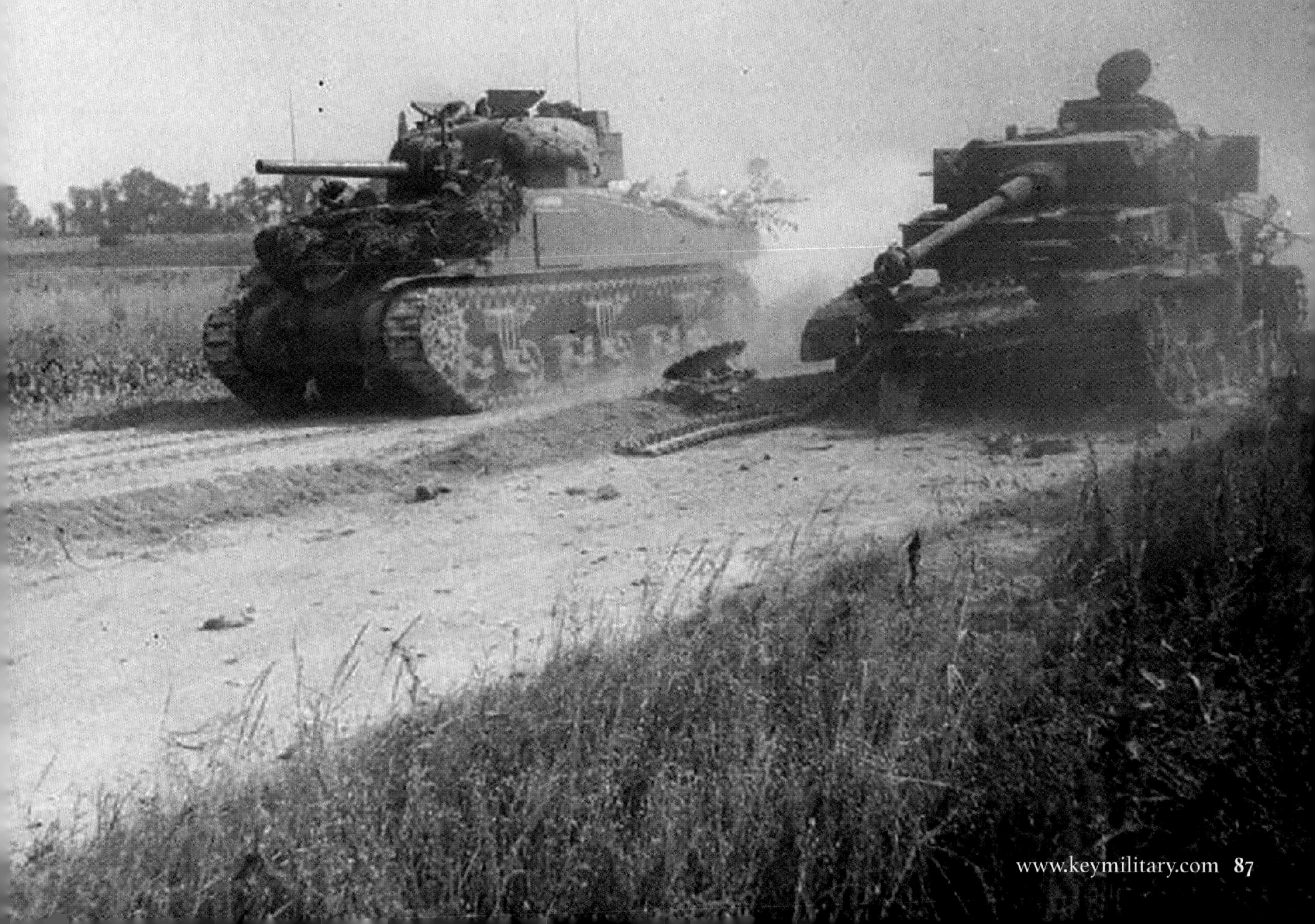

Killing Michael Wittman

The infamous German panzer ace met his end at the muzzle of a British tank gun

SS-Oberführer Kurt 'Panzer' Meyer watched two British armoured divisions preparing for battle on the late morning of 8 August 1944. Concealed in the upper story of a French barn in Normandy, he saw tanks, halftracks and carriers spread out before him in an awesome display of firepower. He knew the battered German forces in the area could not defend against such an onslaught. Since they could not defend, he decided they would attack. Meyer hoped such a move would disrupt the British attack, allowing time for other German units to arrive and bolster the defence.

The coming British attack was part of Operation Totalise, designed to capture the high ground near the French town of Falaise and help trap German forces in a pocket. Part of this operation involved tank-heavy columns punching through gaps in the German positions and penetrating into their rear areas. Infantry following the tanks would mop up the bypassed German troops. The attack proceeded well, and by midday German lines were pierced in depths up to six km. The British attack paused just after noon, waiting for a massive airstrike using Allied heavy bombers. This unwittingly

gave the Germans a short time to prepare their own counterattack.

The Germans had about 20 tanks from Panzer Regiment 12, mostly Panzer IVs. They also had the heavy Tiger I tanks of the 2nd Company, SS Heavy Tank Battalion 101, commanded by Hauptsturmführer Michael Wittmann. The Nazi propaganda machine made a national hero of Wittman due to his skill against enemy tanks. Wittmann served two years in the German army before joining the SS, where he saw

combat in Poland, the Balkans and the Soviet Union before being promoted to officer rank.

Joining a Tiger tank unit in December 1942, he fought at Kursk and was transferred to the Normandy area in January 1944. On 13 June 1944, Wittmann's company mauled a British column at Villers-Bocage, adding to his reputation. By 8 August 1944 he is believed to have destroyed as many as 139 Allied tanks.

As Meyer gave Wittmann his orders, they saw a single Allied bomber fly

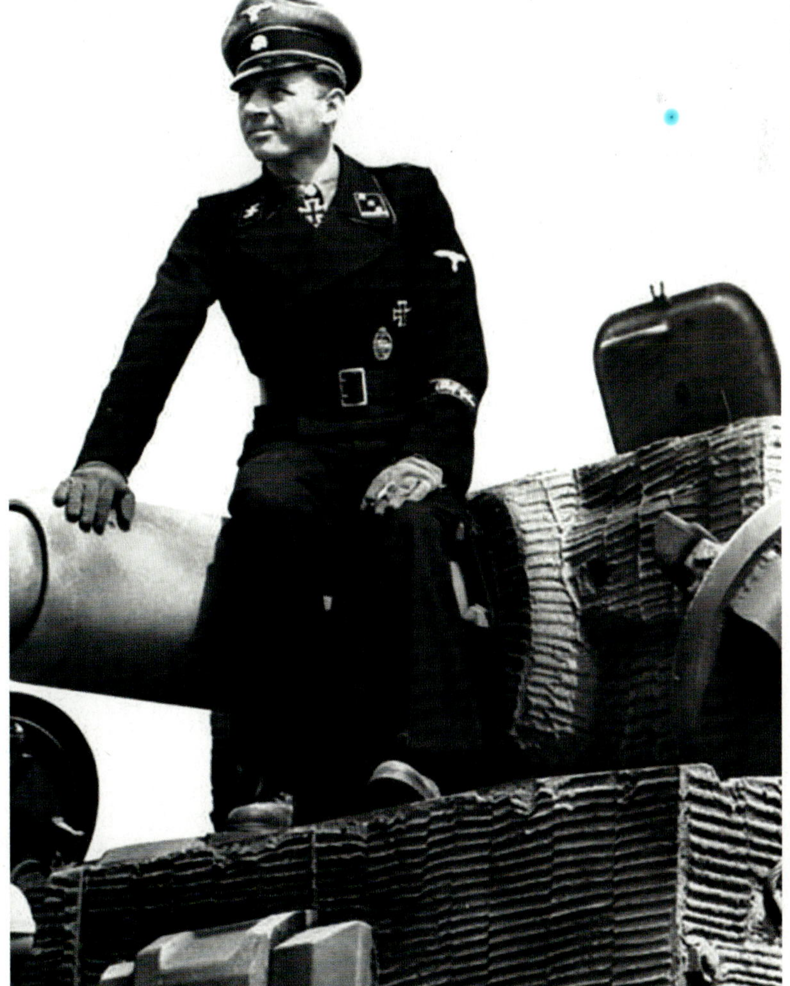

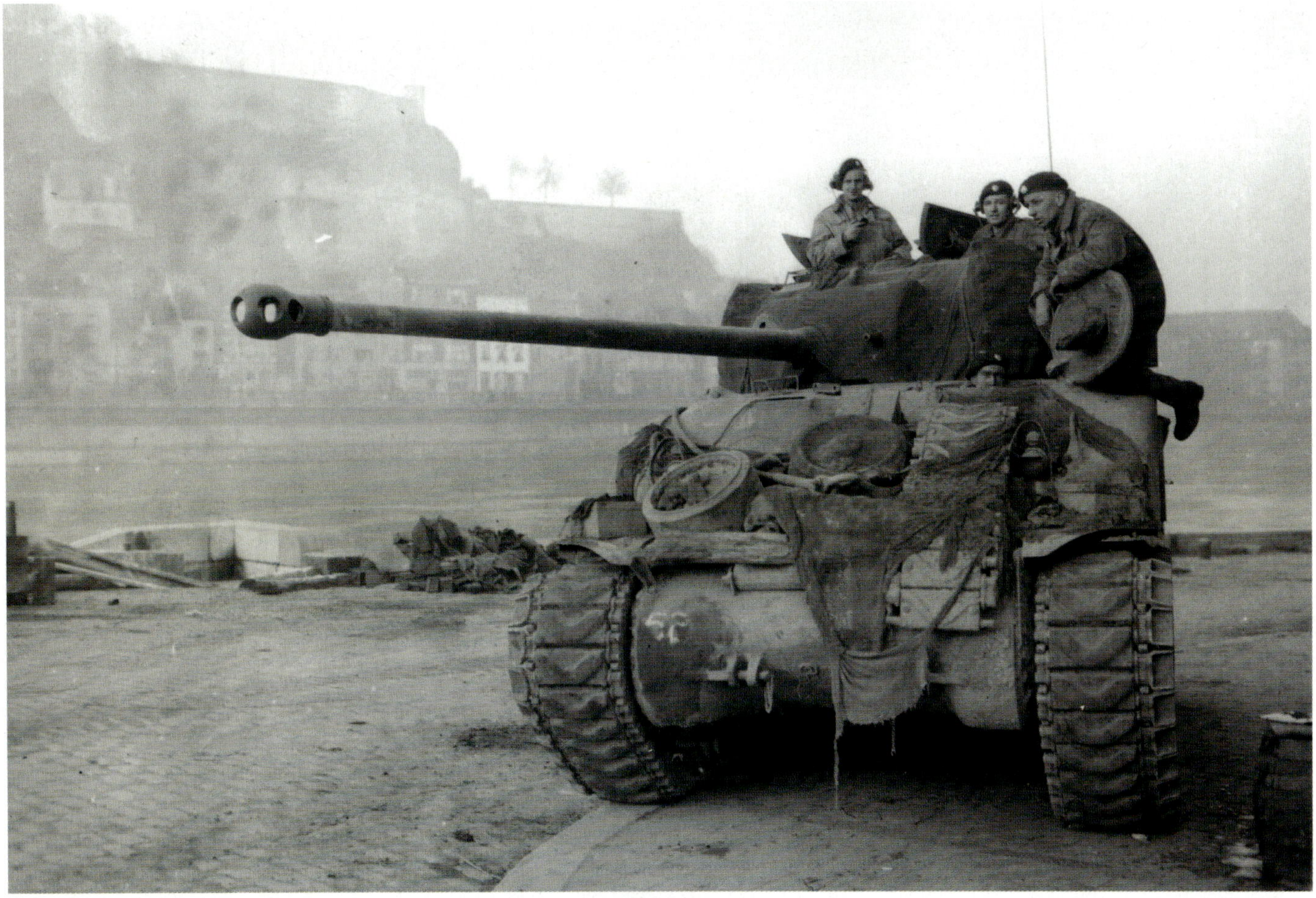

over, dropping a line of flares. They knew this meant a heavy air attack was coming within a few minutes; they had to attack now. Wittmann gathered the four Tigers he had available and advanced, commanding from Tiger 007. His normal tank, Tiger 205, was down for repairs.

Across the battlefield, the 1st Northamptonshire Yeomanry sat in some orchards south of the town of St. Aignan. This unit used the Sherman tank, most equipped with the short 75mm cannon. A few were Sherman Fireflies, carrying a long, high velocity 17-pounder gun. A similarly equipped unit, the Canadian Sherbrooke Fusiliers, sat to the northwest. Wittmann's small column of Tigers came toward both units from the south.

British artillery fire fell all around the four Tigers as they advanced in a column, but none were knocked out. The Sherbrooke Fusiliers exchanged fire with Wittmann's tanks at long range, about 1800m. The Tiger crews managed to hit several Shermans before continuing north. Just then the Allied bombers arrived, the sky filled with them. One German soldier quipped, "What an honour! Churchill is sending a bomber for each of us!" German troops fled their positions as hundreds of bombs fell.

Wittmann's Tigers kept going, soon coming into view of 3 Troop,

ABOVE: The Firefly's long barrel made it more noticeable on the battlefield. German tank gunners would target a Firefly due to the threat it posed to German armour. (US NATIONAL ARCHIVES)

LEFT: Michael Wittmann sitting on the mantlet of a Tiger I tank in Northern France, early 1944. The textured lines on the tank's armour is Zimmerit paste, applied to prevent magnetic charges being attached to the vehicle. (BUNDESARCHIV)

ABOVE: Tiger Is of Michael Wittman's 2nd Company SS Heavy Panzer Battalion 101, advance down a French road. Tiger I production ceased in August 1944 in favour of the larger Tiger II. (US NATIONAL ARCHIVES)

RIGHT: This US soldier examines a knocked-out Tiger. A Firefly could penetrate a Tiger I's side armour from beyond 2,000m, while a 75mm armed Sherman had to be within 100m. (US NATIONAL ARCHIVES)

A Squadron of the Northamptonshire Yeomanry. The troop had three standard Shermans and one Firefly, commanded by Sgt. Gordon. He and his troop commander, Lt. James, spotted the Tigers at 1,200m. Captain Boardman, squadron second in command, soon arrived. The Germans seemed unaware of 3 Troop's presence, so they waited until the Tigers closed the range to 800m and were moving perpendicular to the British, exposing their thinner side armour. The Firefly could penetrate the Tiger's armour as this distance, so Sgt. Gordon ordered his Firefly forward, just slightly out of the trees, to improve its field of fire. It was 12:39 PM.

Gordon kept his head out of the hatch for better visibility but could see only three of the Tigers. He told his gunner, Joe Ekins, to fire at the rear Tiger; with luck, its comrades would not notice right away, giving them a few more seconds of engagement time. Ekins felt nervous, engaging a column of Tigers, but he later recalled also thinking 'Get the bastard before he gets you." He took careful aim.

The 17-pounder gun created a lot of pressure inside the turret when it fired. The rest of the crew covered their ears, closed their eyes and opened their mouths to reduce the effect. Gordon gave the order and Ekins pressed his foot on the floor-mounted firing button for the main gun. With a thunderous roar and a bright muzzle flash, the armour-piercing rounds flew toward the Tiger at nearly 1,000m per second.

The loader immediately pushed another round into the cannon and Ekins fired again. Both rounds hit and within seconds the Tiger was burning. Gordon ordered the driver to reverse back into the trees to avoid return fire. As they moved, the turret of the second Tiger in line swung toward them. Seconds later an 88mm round flew past, barely missing the Firefly. Two more rounds went by as the British tank disappeared into the wood.

In chaos of the moment, Sgt. Gordon was wounded when his hatch crashed down on his head. Whether this was causing by an 88mm round, a tree branch or the tank's movement is unknown, but Gordon was out of the fight, also taking shrapnel from a nearby German artillery burst.

The Firefly had the best chance on knocking out the remaining Tigers, so Lt. James ran through the German shellfire to take command of it. He ordered the driver to move to a new firing position, something a well-trained crew automatically did. Within a few minutes they were ready for another shot at the Germans. James told the driver to pull forward so they could see their opponents. Ekins took aim at the tank which had just fired at them. Focused as he was on hitting the tank in its side armour, Ekins likely did not see the number 007 on the Tiger's turret.

Pushing down his foot on the firing button, Ekins fired. The muzzle flash and dust blinded the crew for a moment, and they worried whether they hit the target. Within a few moments, the air cleared, however, revealing the Tiger, smoke rising from it. A few seconds later the tank exploded in a cloud of flame and smoke. Tiger 007's ammunition detonated, throwing the turret high into the air. They could not have known at the time, but the British crews had just ended the life of one of Germany's most famous tank aces. Ekins didn't know about Wittmann until years after the war.

Lt. James ordered the Firefly back into cover, but the other British Shermans opened fire on the remaining Tiger with their 75mm guns. The location of the fourth Tiger was unknown to them at the time. Numerous rounds struck the Tiger, but it remained operational. The crews seemed to be rattled, however, as the tank began to move rapidly and change directions. A British observer remarked the Tiger appeared to be "milling around wondering how he could escape."

The Firefly moved back out to fire again. Accounts differ; Ekins recalled putting two rounds into it, causing the tank to catch fire. Capt. Boardman's tank may have managed to penetrate it as well. Whatever the case the Tiger was finished. The engagement ended at 12:52 PM; in less than 15 minutes three irreplaceable Tigers were lost, possibly by a single tank using only five rounds of ammunition.

This account of Wittmann's demise is the generally accepted one, although some claim a tank from the Sherbrooke Fusiliers fired the fatal shot at Wittmann's Tiger 007. Other tanks were shooting at the Germans as well, and in the chaos of combat it can be very difficult to tell who hit a particular tank. German accounts note only one Tiger, 007, lost its turret when hit that day.

Knocking out Wittmann's column of Tigers was a group effort by several units and which tank struck the killing blow was ultimately not important. The account is an excellent example of the advantage of a tank crew when it spots the enemy first and gets off the first accurate shot.

Ekins survived the war and generally stayed out of the arguments around who killed Wittmann. He never claimed to be solely responsible for it. Interviewed shortly before his death in 2012, Ekins stated, seemingly without bitterness, that Wittmann, having willingly served Hitler and the Nazi regime, got the fate he deserved. The Northamptonshire Yeomanry's war diary summed up the action by relating the most important part of the outcome: "Three Tigers in twelve minutes is not bad business."

BELOW: A Sherman Firefly in Normandy, using a treeline for partial concealment. The 17-pounder gun produced a large muzzle flash and sound when firing, so the crew would move quickly after shooting. (US NATIONAL ARCHIVES)

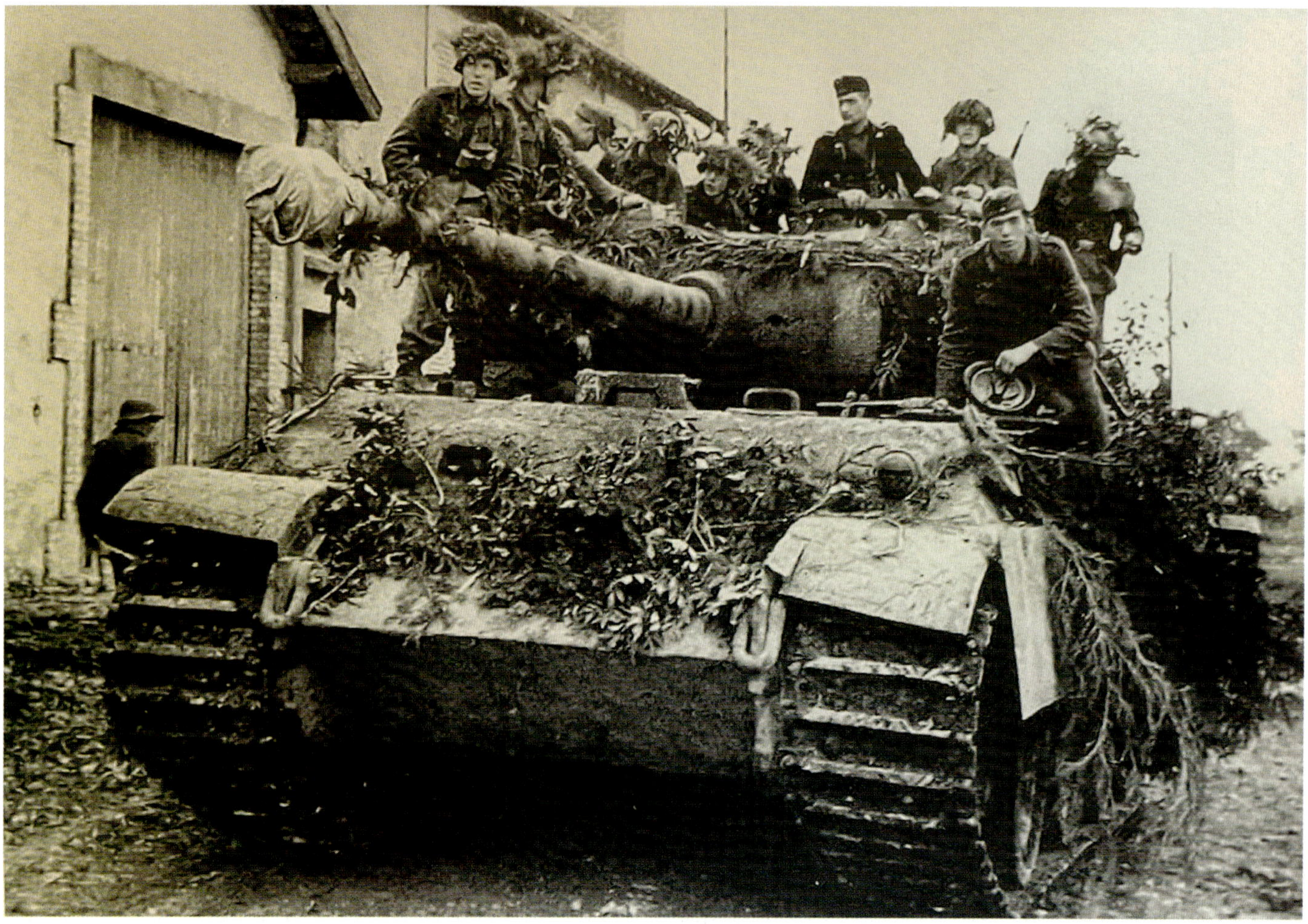

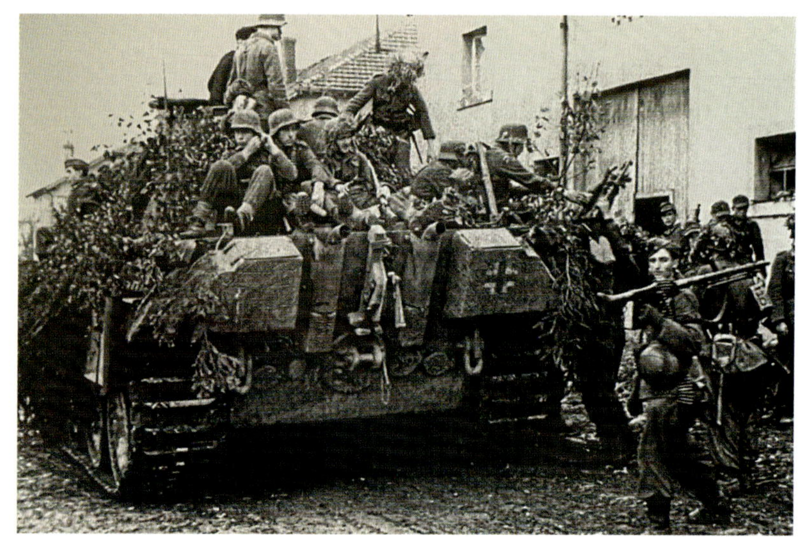

Arracourt

US 4th Armored Division's victory in France

ABOVE: A Panther tank of Panzer Brigade 111. The camouflage on the tank was mainly useful for hiding in wooded areas to avoid Allied aircraft. (BUNDESARCHIV BILD 101L-301-1955-22/KURTH/CC-BY-SA-3.0)

After the Allies broke out of the Normandy beachhead they advanced quickly toward the German border. The German units which fought in Normandy were wrecked and posed little threat to the spearheads of the well supplied and highly mechanised US Third Army, commanded by General George Patton.

The Germans desperately tried to assemble a force to stop the American advance. Newly formed Panzer Brigades (PBs) rushed to the front. These units had a mix of panzer and panzergrenadier (mechanised infantry) battalions along with an assault gun, reconnaissance, and engineer companies.

On paper these brigades looked impressive, but they lacked organic artillery and maintenance assets critical to successful armoured operations. Experienced German field commanders like Gen. Hasso von Manteuffel considered them improvised units created due to shortages of men and new equipment. Their subunits were brought together from different areas and thrown into combat without time to train or learn to work together. Hitler, always excited by new concepts, wanted them, however, and so they marched west to meet the Americans.

The American unit they met coming the other way was the 4th Armored Division. Led by able and aggressive officers and equipped with the M4 Sherman and M5 Stuart tanks, it raced across France after leaving Normandy. Its pursuit of the German units retreating from Normandy and Southern France allowed it to gain practical battle experience while not suffering high attrition through set battles.

RIGHT: Panzergrenadiers of the 211th Regiment mount a Panther on 20 September for an attack at Arracourt. High losses of halftracks and trucks forced many troops to ride on the tanks. (BUNDESARCHIV BILD 101L-301-1955-15/KURTH/CC-BY-SA 3.0)

Twenty of its Shermans carried the 76mm gun, which had better anti-armour performance. However, most of the leaders in 4th Armored preferred the 75mm-armed Sherman as its gun had a better high-explosive round. Patton thought tanks should attack enemy infantry and artillery and conduct breakthroughs into the enemy's rear areas. He discouraged the idea of tank versus tank fighting, preferring to destroy panzer formations with air support, artillery and anti-tank units. War is chaotic, however, and sometimes tank fighting occurred anyway.

The panzer brigades of German 1st Army and 5th Panzer Army and the US 4th Armored Division met in the eastern French province of Lorraine in September 1944. These actions took place over a wide area, but the fighting has generally become known as the Battle of Arracourt. At this point the US advance suffered from lack of fuel, causing it to slow and even stop in some places.

The opening round occurred around the town of Mairy on 7 September. Panther tanks and Jagdpanzer IV tank destroyers of PB106, commanded by Col. Franz Bake and supported by panzergrenadiers, attacked near the town of Briey, east of Mairy. US 4th Armored was south of this area, so the attack ran into the US 90th Infantry Division, supported by the 712th Tank Battalion and 607th Tank Destroyer Battalion, equipped with towed 76mm anti-tank guns.

Moving at night, the Panthers drove right past the 90th's headquarters tents, protected by A Company of the 712th. When the Panthers stopped to investigate, the Americans opened fire. Tanks on both sides burst into flames, illuminating the battlefield for other tank gunners. The fighting turned into an attack on the command post. An American maintenance officer jumped in a Sherman down for repair and knocked out a Panther. Repulsed, the German force turned toward Mairy but ran into a storm of bazooka, artillery and anti-tank fire. One poorly trained German tank crew surrendered when American infantry threw hand grenades at it. Panzer Brigade 106 retreated with heavy losses.

The next Panzer attack came at Lunéville on 18 September. The Panthers of PB111 quickly pushed through the 4th Armored's cavalry screen of light tanks and armoured cars. Afterward, they ran into M18 tank destroyers and lost three tanks. Lt. Richard Buss, commanding an M18 platoon, recalled one of

ABOVE: The M18 Hellcat tank destroyer looked different from previous models, so they were put on display for advancing American troops as a recognition aid. The muzzle brake is painted red to help with distant recognition. (US NATIONAL ARCHIVES)

LEFT: The shattered hulk of a Panzer IV near Juvelize. It is believed a P-47 airstrike destroyed this tank. (US NATIONAL ARCHIVES)

his men putting two rounds into a Panther with no immediate reaction. Then, "I saw billowing flames. It was not the dramatic kind of explosion that one would have expected. The flames were transparent orange, rising with a startling swiftness. They rose through the branches of the trees to a height of nearly sixty feet."

Despite support from PB112, the Germans attack failed through the actions of two combat commands of 4th Armored. A combination of tanks, tank destroyers and artillery pushed the Germans back with the loss of at least 21 tanks. This defeat did not deter the Germans from launching their next attack around Arracourt the next morning, 19 September.

That attack began in a dense early morning fog which played against the Germans. Most of the Panther's superiority over the Sherman came from its advantages at long range combat. The fog reduced the ranges at which enemy tanks could be spotted and engaged, evening the odds. Task forces from 4th Armored's CCA sat at strategic points north and east of Arracourt, supported by artillery, infantry and scouts.

PB113 led the German attack against these units, but several groups of German troops blundered into US outposts and were captured. This gave the Americans warning of the impending panzer assault. Soon Panther tanks appeared out of the fog and the American screening units pulled back, with the Germans following.

A platoon of M18 tank destroyers set up on a hill near Rechicourt just as the lead German tank platoons left a fog bank. The Americans opened fire, knocking out five Panthers for the loss of a single M18. The platoon changed position and spotted a column of Panzer IVs, hitting 6 or 7 in the ensuing action, but losing two more M18s. Above, Maj. Charles Carpenter, flying a small artillery observation plane, also joined the fight. Known as

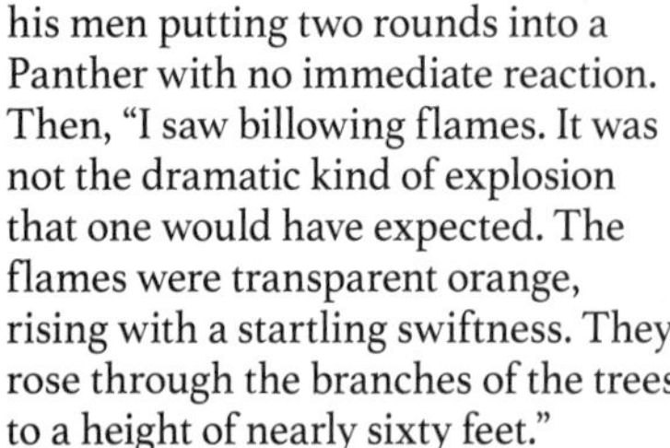

'Bazooka Charlie,' Carpenter had six bazookas mounted on the wings of his spotter plane and used them to attack the German armour.

The German column next met C Company, 37th Tank Battalion which knocked out two Panthers and forced the column to fall back. The US company commander, Capt. Kenneth Lamison, took a platoon to a nearby hill and destroyed four more Panthers, reversed to hide behind the hill, then emerged to shoot the last four Panthers in the formation as they withdrew. Another attack, possibly by PB111, also failed, driven back by an American task force of

Shermans and M18s. This attack went in at ranges as close as 250m, destroying eight German tanks and 100 supporting infantry.

The next day saw more German attacks, even though one German estimate put 45 operational panzers against 130 Shermans. CCA was actually beginning its own attack when PB111 appeared, firing on the CCA command post and a nearby artillery battalion. The US 155mm howitzers used heavy explosive shells to cripple two panzers and force the rest back.

The US 37th Tank Battalion pushed ahead with its attack but ran into an ambush, losing six Shermans. Later in the day the 37th's tanks made a massed night attack on the German position at Moncourt, recorded in its diary: "The whole formation opened fire as one… the storm of incendiary bullets and high explosive set Moncourt afire as forces moved in, grinding under the opposition…"

From 21-23 September the fighting shifted to the area around Juvelize, where another early-morning panzer attack blew through the American screens of light tanks but suffered badly at the hands of the experienced Sherman crews and P-47 Thunderbolt fighter-bombers, appearing over the battlefield as the weather improved. By the end PB111 had only seven tanks

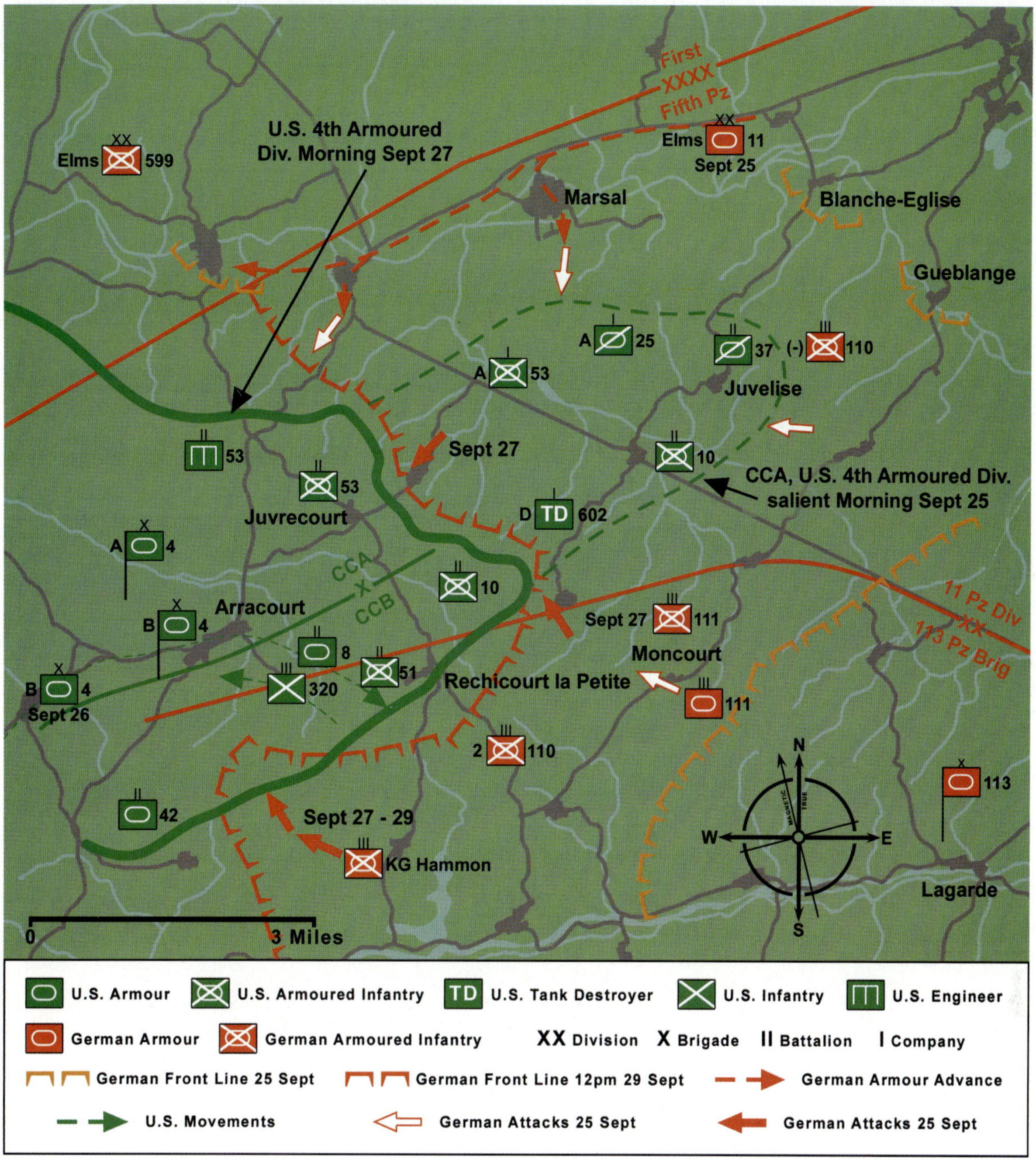

Legend

- U.S. Armour
- U.S. Armoured Infantry
- TD U.S. Tank Destroyer
- U.S. Infantry
- U.S. Engineer
- German Armour
- German Armoured Infantry
- XX Division
- X Brigade
- II Battalion
- I Company
- German Front Line 25 Sept
- German Front Line 12pm 29 Sept
- German Armour Advance
- U.S. Movements
- German Attacks 25 Sept
- German Attacks 25 Sept

BELOW: A knocked-out Sherman of the 4th Armored Division on 27 September 1944. The unit preferred the versatility of the 75mm armed Sherman over the specialised anti-tank performance of the longer 76mm gun. (US NATIONAL ARCHIVES)

and 80 men left from an original force of 90 tanks and 2,500 troops.

The rest of September saw heavy fighting as the German attempted to pierce American positions around Arracourt. Ultimately, this effort resulted in a stalemate due to German exhaustion and losses. The Third Army, using primarily the 4th Armored Division, blunted the efforts of two German field armies and several of the new panzer brigades, causing casualties and tank losses the Germans could not afford. The battles around Arracourt comprised one of the few large-scale tank battles in Western Europe before the Ardennes fighting in December 1944. It showed the growing expertise of American troops and the waning quality of German units, along with the inability of Germany to properly supply and train them. The end of Hitler's Reich was in sight.

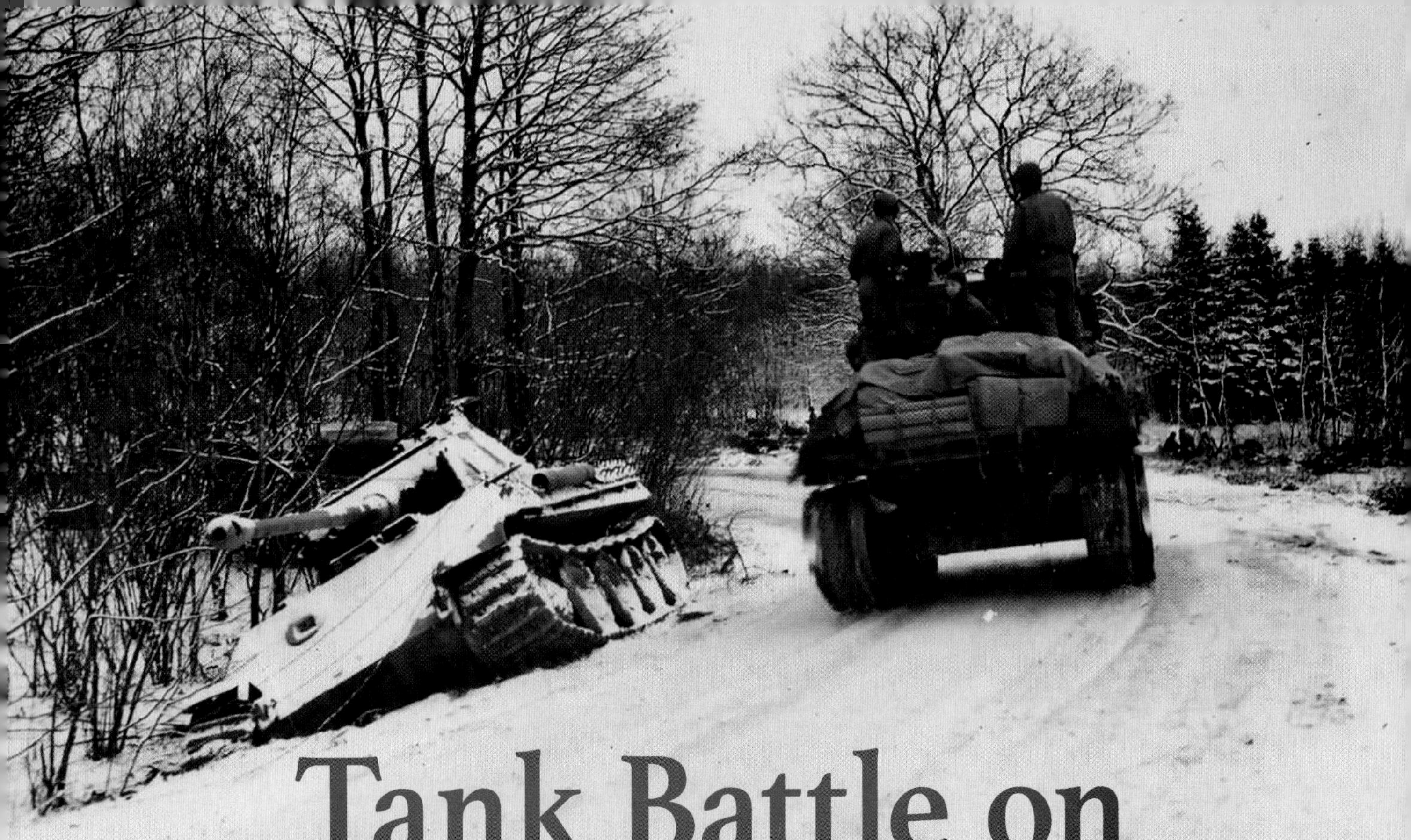

Tank Battle on Christmas Eve

Panthers versus Shermans on a snowy battlefield

ABOVE: Tanks knocked out on roads were quickly pushed off to the side to clear the way for advancing forces. The US Sherman passes a destroyed Panther a few miles north of Freyneaux. (US NATIONAL ARCHIVES)

The Battle of the Bulge remains the largest battle ever fought by the U.S. Army, involving 610,000 US troops, of which 81,000 became casualties. The last large-scale tank battle of the war in Western Europe, it saw the employment of Nazi Germany's last armour reserves. Like any large battle, it was really the amalgamation of hundreds of smaller battles linked by common purpose.

One such small action took place in the Belgian village of Freyneaux on Christmas Eve, 1944. A tiny hamlet of 130 people, in 1944 it had a church, a small cemetery and a few clusters of stout stone homes and shops which mainly served the surrounding farms. Several local roads converged at Freyneaux, which made it worthy of defending. Here, soldiers of the defending US 3rd Armored Division faced attack by the German 2nd SS Panzer Division *'Das Reich.'*

American Major Robert Coughlin commanded the defences at Freyneaux. He used the village's buildings and walls as cover for his troops; clumps of trees dotted Freyneaux, providing some concealment. A road led northeast from the village to a small stone bridge over the narrow River Aisne. Beyond the bridge was north-south road connecting other villages in the area.

Coughlin knew other American units covered the west, so he oriented most of his troops to defend toward the east. A pair of M4 Shermans and a pair of M5 Stuarts guarded two roads leading southeast and southwest from Freyneaux. Three Shermans protected the northeastern approaches. D-31, an M4A3 (76mm), belonged to 1st Lt. Charles Myers. It sat at the edge of the village near the church. Just north of the road leading to the bridge stood Sgt. Alvin Beckmann's D-34, armed with a short 75mm cannon, concealed between a barn and a large woodpile. D-32, another M4A3 (76mm) commanded

RIGHT: An equipment laden M5 Stuart follows a column of Shermans. The Stuart was almost useless against German armour but its small cannon and 3 machine guns were effective against enemy infantry. (US NATIONAL ARCHIVES)

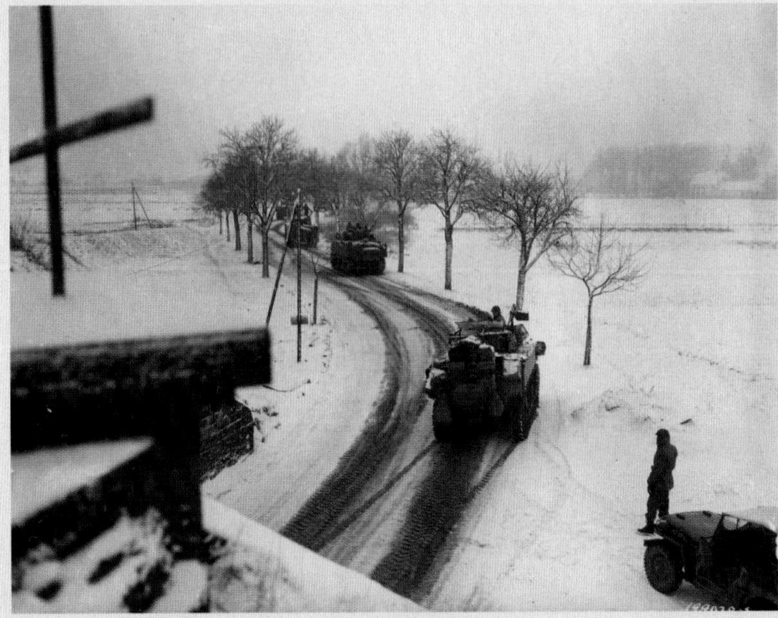

Due to their delay, the Germans approached Freyneaux without doing proper reconnaissance and did not know the village was actually well-defended. Most of the Panthers had infantry riding on their engine decks. *Untersturmführer* Fritz Langanke commanded the lead platoon of four tanks. An SS veteran who had personally destroyed 19 tanks, Langanke was assigned to clear Freyneaux.

They turned off the north-south road and neared the bridge east of the village. Langanke saw something on the bridge which looked like a mine and became suspicious. He moved the platoon a short distance north of the bridge and found a spot where the riverbed seemed firm enough to support the weight of a 50-ton Panther. They crossed there while Hargesheimer and the rest of the panzer company crossed the river south of the bridge and took up positions overlooking the village.

Forming a line to maximise firepower, Langanke led his four tanks across a hilly field toward Freyneaux. They saw no enemy presence, but the Americans heard their engines and were ready. When the Germans appeared, moving down a small hill, they presented their thinner side armour to D-31. The gunner, Corp. Jim Vance, judged the range at less than 500m. He took careful aim and depressed the firing pedal of the Sherman's cannon with his foot. The 76mm high-velocity round flew from the barrel and crashed into one of the Panthers, setting it ablaze. The crew bailed out and all the German infantry leapt from the engine decks of the Panthers.

Vance fired again and a second Panther burst into flames. He saw the third tank take a hit from another ❯

by Sgt. Reece Graham, set up behind a high stone wall which concealed all but the turret of his tank. A pair of Stuarts, two 76mm anti-tank guns and about 45 dismounted reconnaissance troops supported the Shermans.

The cold weather meant the tank crewmen took turns sitting watch in their tank while the rest of the crew sheltered in nearby homes. They knew the Germans were close and expected an attack at any time. Shivering in a tank turret was better than being surprised.

A few miles east, those Germans were indeed preparing an attack. *Obersturmführer* Alfred Hargesheimer commanded 2nd Company, SS Panzer Regiment 2, equipped with Panther medium tanks. Luck turned against them in their first plan, to attack Freyneaux just before midnight on 23 December. On the way there, several tanks became stuck in a swampy area. It took hours to free them, so the attack was rescheduled for the morning of the 24th. The Germans expected Freyneaux to be only

lightly defended; their main force was actually on the way to a larger target and planned to simply dispatch a small force to clear the village as they passed.

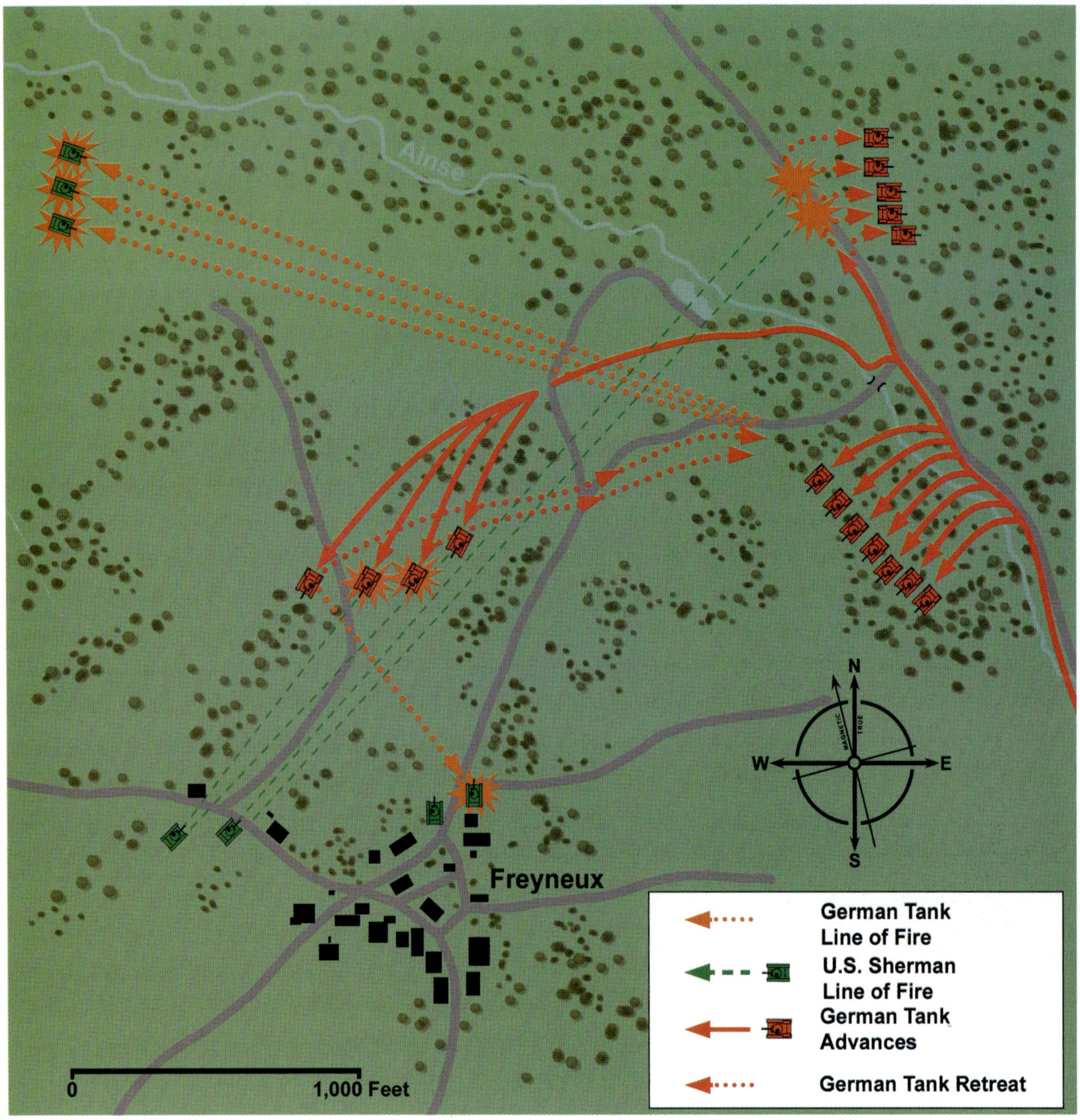

BELOW: Another knocked out Panther near Grandmenil. American tank crews respected the Panther's firepower and frontal armour but knew its side armour was vulnerable even at long range. (US NATIONAL ARCHIVES)

US tank, so he sought out the fourth Panther. Langanke began searching for the attacker who had destroyed half his platoon in seconds. He spotted D-31 and his gunner fired a round which hit the stonewall the Sherman sheltered behind. Unable to locate their opponent, D-31 backed behind the church.

Meanwhile, Sgt. Beckmann's D-34 refused to start, affected by the cold.

As the crew traversed the turret to engage Langanke's Panther, they were spotted. Only 100 yards away, Langanke gunner put a round into D-34's turret, starting a fire. The crew bailed out except for the driver; his hatch was jammed partway open, trapping him. In desperation he stripped off all his winter clothing, enabling him to squeeze out. In his underwear, he ran to a nearby house and took cover.

Langanke's tank also fired at D-32, which had taken cover behind a wall. The two tanks exchanged fire without a hit, but then Sgt. Graham spotted another group of Panthers moving up the north-south road across the river. It was a German unit moving toward the next objective, unaware they were under American observation and presenting their rear armour to the American tank. Graham ordered his gunner to engage them even though the range was around 2,000m. Their second shot set a Panther on fire. The third shot did the same.

The remaining three Panthers turned east into the forest to escape the murderous American fire.

Before Langanke could move his tank for a better shot, his Panther began taking fire from a new direction. The two US anti-tank guns joined the battle and soon round after round slammed into the Panther. Ten rounds hit the frontal armour; none of them penetrated but the welds in the armour plate cracked. Langanke sprayed the area with machine gun fire, but an eleventh round hit the turret and bounced away, a fragment of it hitting Langanke in the head. Knocked senseless, when he came around he decided his crew had risked enough and ordered the driver to back away, keeping the frontal armour facing the incoming enemy fire.

Using every low spot in the terrain the Panther got away, taking cover in the woods near the third tank from his platoon, damaged but not destroyed in the opening volleys. Nearby, Hargesheimer led his remaining seven Panthers towards the village. They left the wood and spotted a single M5 Stuart, which they quickly destroyed. Several Shermans in the town moved to engage this new threat. One of the crewmen of the destroyed Stuart found a good firing position and led one of the Shermans to it. That crew hit a Panther, by luck Hargesheimer's tank, disabling the main gun and wounding the loader.

Hargesheimer realised he was losing too many tanks and ordered a withdrawal back to the trees. One Panther was destroyed and another immobilised on the way, leaving only four operational. The situation for the Germans worsened when the weather cleared, and American fighter-bombers appeared overhead.

Cpl. Vance watched the planes drop bombs, and strafe with machine guns, calling it "a beautiful sight."

An American lieutenant climbed the church's steeple, hoping to direct artillery fire on the Germans. As the US artillery opened fire, the Germans spotted him and put several rounds into the steeple, blowing it apart. The German infantry moved to the edge of town and tried to attack the Americans with panzerfausts. The American tank crews spotted them and turned their machine guns on the anti-tank teams, gunning them all down, though the Germans managed to destroy another M5 Stuart.

The German troops withdrew from Freyneaux and the battle seemed to be winding down, but there was one more action. A German tank gunner spotted five Shermans on a hill north of Freyneaux, about 1,000m away. These tanks belonging to the neighbouring US 9th Armored Division and were trying to return to their own unit, unaware of the fighting in Freyneaux.

The gunner fired, striking the first Sherman in its gun, spraying the tank commander with fragments. Within seconds more rounds crashed into the hapless Shermans, set the first one afire and knocking out three more. The fifth tank managed to retreat back over the hill. The Christmas Eve battle for Freyneaux was over.

The fighting was costly to both sides. The Americans lost five Shermans and two Stuarts while the Germans lost five Panthers with several more damaged. Importantly, the successful US defence delayed the German plans to capture towns in the area, another small loss which cumulated in German defeat in the Battle of the Bulge.

LEFT: The crew of an M5 Stuart pour machine gun fire at enemy troops in a wooded area. German infantry at Freyneaux suffered heavily from American machine gun fire. (US NATIONAL ARCHIVES)

BELOW: A Panther advances down a snowy road in the Ardennes. This tank has extra track links on the side to bolster armour protection. (BUNDESARCHIV)

Drive to Bastogne

The US 4th Armored Division's deadly race to the besieged city

The German offensive into the Ardennes in December 1944 took the Allies by surprise. A desperate gamble by Hitler designed to drive a physical wedge between the American and British armies, it drove deep into lines held by four exhausted or inexperienced infantry divisions. While some looked at it as a dire threat, Supreme Allied Commander Dwight Eisenhower saw it as an opportunity. The Germans had stuck their proverbial necks out and Eisenhower hoped to stick a bayonet into it.

US General George Patton, volatile but skilled, said he could turn his Third Army north from its current location, move 100 miles and hit the Germans in their southern flank in just two days. It meant cancelling plans for his own offensive, yet Patton quipped, "But what the hell, we'll still be killing

RIGHT: Sgt. John H. Parks commanded a Sherman tank in the 37th Tank Battalion. He was killed in the hatch of his tank near Flatzbourhof on 23 December, 1944. (US NATIONAL ARCHIVES)

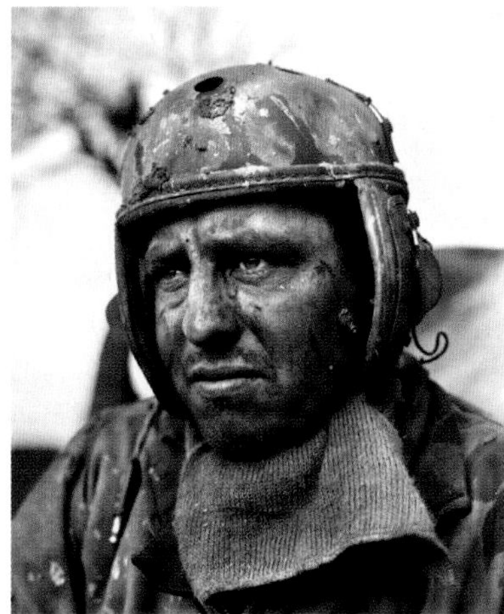

Krauts." Patton assigned his best units to lead the attack, which aimed to relieve the surrounded American units at the crossroads town of Bastogne.

The point of the bayonet now aimed at the advancing Germans was the 4th Armored Division under Maj. Gen. Hugh Gaffey. A 'triangular' armoured division, it organised its units into three Combat Commands (CC), designated A, B and R (for Reserve). Each had a tank battalion, a battalion of infantry mounted in halftracks, and a self-propelled howitzer battalion, plus attached detachments of engineers, tank destroyers, medics and scouts. Combat Commands could move fast and hit hard.

The main German unit standing in the path of 4th Armored was Fallschirmjaeger Division 5, a paratrooper unit acting as regular infantry. Supporting the infantry were artillery, anti-tank, engineer, and anti-aircraft troops with a mortar battalion. An understrength brigade of Sturmgeschutz assault guns increased their firepower.

Gen. Gaffey assigned CCA to be the main effort, as it had the most

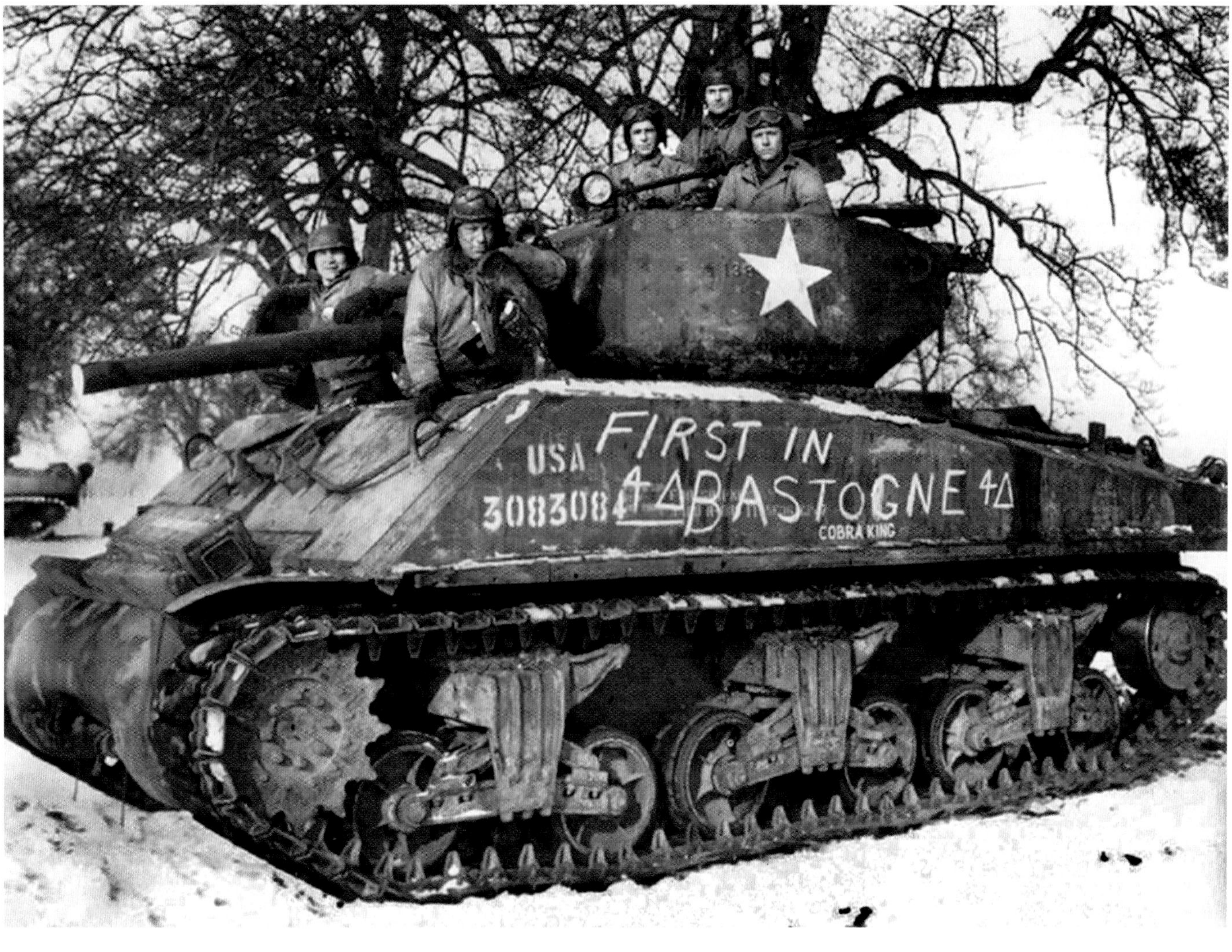

BELOW: The first tank to break through to Bastogne was Cobra King, a heavy M4A3E2 assault tank. Today it sits on display at the National Museum of the United States Army at Fort Belvoir, Virginia (US NATIONAL ARCHIVES)

operational tanks in the division. CCB advanced to their left and CCR stayed behind in reserve until the situation forced their commitment. Just after dawn a reconnaissance unit of CCB ran into the Germans at Chaumont, exchanging heavy fire. The battle to get to Bastogne was underway.

The advance began slowly, as the worsening weather brought blowing snow which reduced visibility and made the roads treacherous. The columns discovered another problem; as American units retreated from the attacking Germans they blew up bridges to slow the German advance. Now 4th Armored needed those river crossings and often had to wait for their engineers to repair them or build new ones.

At 11 AM on 23 December, cavalry scouts of CCA found German troops dug in at Flatzbourhof, Luxembourg and soon became embroiled in a stiff battle. Another unit ran into the Germans at Martelange, a few kilometres west. Infantry went into the town with the tanks in support. When the tanks reached the first intersection, the Germans opened fire with machine guns and panzerfausts. When the fighting stalemated, the US commander sent a platoon of tanks and infantry to flank the German position. Arriving undetected after dark, they blasted the enemy strongholds with cannon fire.

To the west, CCB's main force arrived near Chaumont and found it needed to bridge the Sauer River. While the engineers worked, CCB's commander used tanks to secure the crossing sight and artillery to pummel the nearby German positions. As soon as the bridge was ready, the tanks refuelled and continued the advance. They pushed into Chaumont, Shermans suppressing the enemy with cannon fire while infantry rooted the Germans out of their positions.

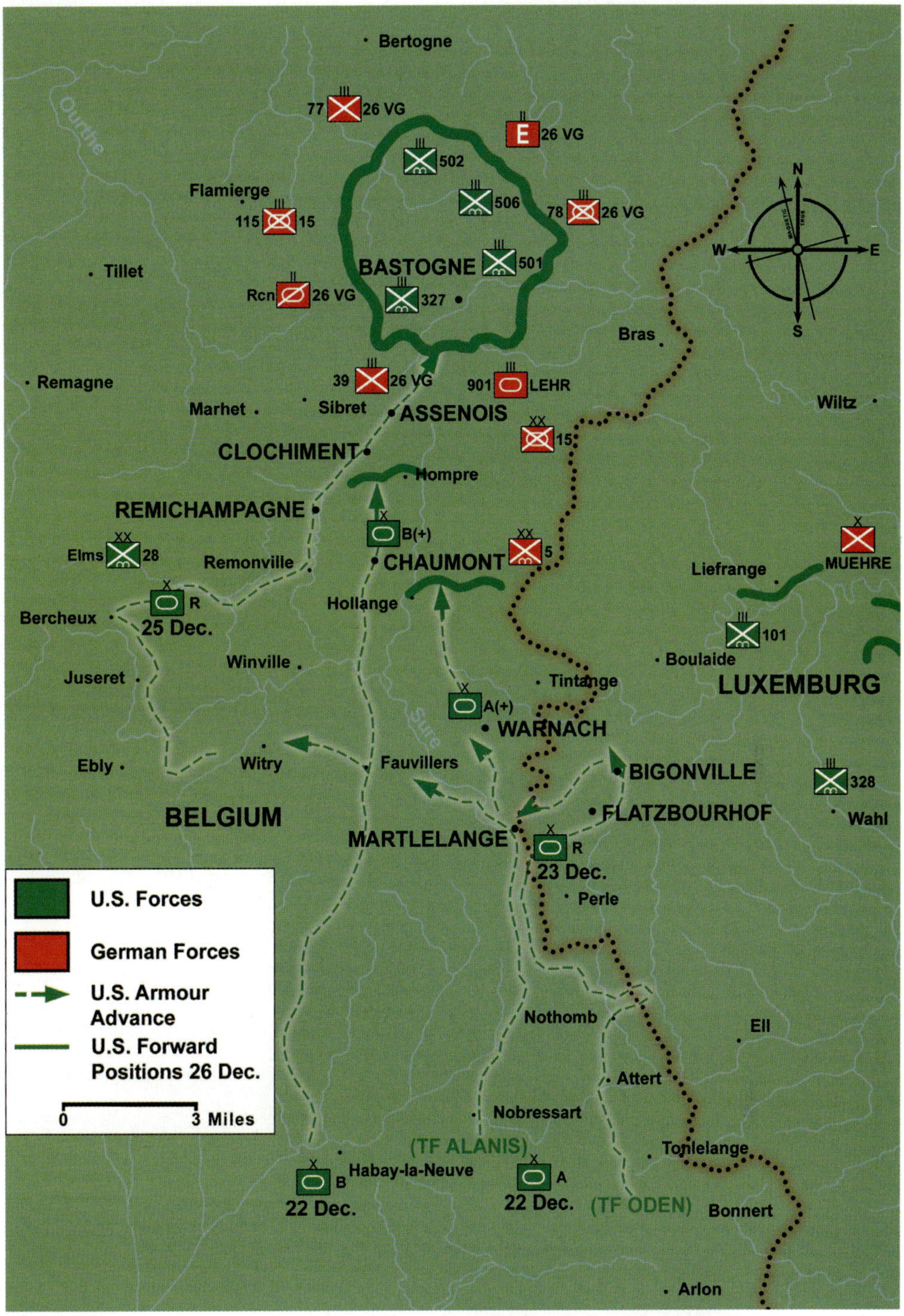

LEFT: A 76mm M4A3 Sherman in the Ardennes. The crew has blacked out the white star on the turret, preventing German gunners from using it as an aiming point. (US NATIONAL ARCHIVES)

ABOVE: A US soldier salvages an MG42 machine gun from a burning StuG III in the Ardennes. Germany was running out of tanks by late 1944 and often substituted assault guns.
(US NATIONAL ARCHIVES)

RIGHT: While modern detractors criticise the Sherman tank, the Germans used every one they captured. The US 37th Tank Battalion destroyed one at Clochimont.
(US NATIONAL ARCHIVES)

RIGHT: Tracked vehicles often have trouble sliding on icy roads. This crew is attaching a device nicknamed a 'duck bill' to their tracks to improve traction.
(US NATIONAL ARCHIVES)

Just as the Americans reached the north end of town and thought the battle finally over, a German counterattack crashed down on them, including assault guns and several Tiger tanks. This force pushed CCB back to the south side of Chaumont, knocking out 11 tanks. Back in Chaumont, the Germans seemed content to hold it and stopped their advance. Infantry would finally clear the town on Christmas Day.

Meanwhile, Gaffey sent CCR to plug a gap between CCA's right flank and the neighbouring US 26th Division. Arriving at Flatzbourhof, Capt. Jimmy Leach of B Company, 37th Tank Battalion sent his tanks in, hearing reports of a captured Sherman in use by the Germans. As they advanced German fire pelted them from trees to the northwest. Sgt. John Parks attacked the enemy while the rest of his platoon provided covering fire. As the Sherman reached the treeline, Parks fell into his hatch, dead from a bullet wound just over his right eye. His gunner took over and started moving the tank to safety but a hit from an assault gun lit the tank on fire. Only two men got out.

Nearby, Capt. Leach spotted the enemy vehicle and the captured Sherman. Moving his tank to a hull down position, the gunner hit the enemy Sherman on his third shot, setting it aflame. The gunner turned his attention to the German assault guns and knocked out two of them. Artillery forced the Germans to retreat, some moving into the town while others fled north. The Germans in Flatzbourhof defended stubbornly, delaying CCR overnight.

CCA met more resistance in Warnach on 23 December. Six US 'assault guns,' Shermans with 105mm howitzers, knocked out German anti-tank guns while M5 Stuart light tanks entered the town.

After dark, German StuG assault guns knocked out these tanks and Shermans went in to engage them. One Sherman gunner, Pfc. Robert Bailey, fired a white phosphorous round into a haystack. The light from the resulting fire revealed the StuG's location. A close-range duel ensued, the Americans losing two Shermans before destroying the StuGs, but their loss broke German morale and they gradually retreated. It took until the afternoon of 24 December, but Warnach fell to CCA.

CCR's 37th Tank battalion, commanded by Lt. Col. Creighton Abrams, used a new tactic at Bigonville, where the Germans defended from stout houses. Each tank fired a 75mm shell with a concrete-piercing fuse, blowing a hole in the wall. The tank crew then sprayed the interior with a .50-calibre machine gun before firing another 75mm shell. The Germans soon surrendered.

Enemy counterattacks built on the division's left flank, so Gen. Gaffey assigned CCR to move there. They arrived to protect that flank on the morning of 25 December. Abrams wanted more than a screening mission, however; he wanted his tanks to reach Bastogne, now only

10km away. As CCR pushed through each village, the tanks maintained the advance while detached infantry cleared it. Tanks rotated through the lead position as US artillery landed just ahead of them to clear the way.

On the morning of 26 December, Abrams resumed his advance, attacking the town of Remichampagne. Capt. Leach's B company rained cannon fire on the town until the German defenders took cover in some nearby woods. This proved a mistake as a flight of P-47 fighter-bombers arrived and smashed the woods with rockets, bombs, and napalm. The tanks pushed through Remichampagne.

Germans defended the next village, Clochimont, with artillery and anti-tank guns. Abrams joined the battle, spotting a German self-propelled gun at 1,000m. his gunner destroyed it with a single shot. Capt. Leach said, "I recommended him for the DSC [Distinguished Service Cross] right there. After all here's the colonel – a lot of colonels stay back at the goddamn flagpole but not Abrams. So he knocked out that gun."

CCR was so close to Bastogne now they watched US cargo planes make a supply drop. Company C of the 37th took the lead, nine tanks commanded by Lt. Charles Boggess, standing in the hatch of an M4A3E2 'Jumbo,' an up-armoured Sherman with up to 177mm of protection. The tank bore the name 'Cobra King.'

The column sprayed fire left and right as they burst through Assenois, the last town before Bastogne. US artillery landed along their flanks to protect them. Some of this artillery landed short, stopping part of the column. Boggess continued with three tanks. They found an enemy pillbox and blasted it. German troops milled around in confusion, apparently not expecting American tanks. "They fell like dominoes," Boggess wrote."

The American tanks reached a line of foxholes, the edge of the US defences of Bastogne. Knowing the Germans were using US vehicles and uniforms, he called to them; "Come out, this is the 4th Armored." Eventually a Lt. Webster of the 101st Airborne came forward and Boggess shook his hand.

4th Armored Division had achieved its objective. More fighting remained to keep the road into Bastogne open, but the Battle of the Bulge ended in German defeat. Abrams would rise to general's rank and have America's current main battle tank, the M1, named for him.

Decades later, Boggess told a reporter, "I believe it is appointed to each man to have a few minutes of glory in his life. Mine lasted four miles and 25 minutes."

US 4TH ARMORED DIVISION ORGANISATION, DECEMBER 1944.
Combat Command A
35th Tank Battalion
51st Armoured Infantry Battalion
66th Armored Field Artillery Battalion
Combat Command B
8th Tank Battalion
10th Armoured Infantry Battalion
22nd Armored Field Artillery Battalion
Combat Command R
37th Tank Battalion
53rd Armoured Infantry Battalion
94th Armored Field Artillery Battalion

LEFT: A soldier examines two penetrations on a Sherman tank by enemy gunfire. German gunners often used the white recognition star as an aiming point. (US NATIONAL ARCHIVES)

BELOW: Anti-tank guns posed the greatest threat to Allied tanks during the war. This 75mm PaK40 was destroyed in Belgium during the Ardennes fighting. (US NATIONAL ARCHIVES)

The Sherman in Soviet Service

RIGHT: Two Shermans of the 9th Guards Mechanised Corps on the streets of Vienna in April 1945. Several days of fighting remained in the city after Loza's raid. (USAMHI)

BELOW: StuG III assault guns move down a muddy track in Hungary in 1945. By this stage of the war German armoured units were lucky to have a half-dozen vehicles available. (US NATIONAL ARCHIVES)

Many accounts of World War Two portray Soviet forces as tactically inept, inflexible, and able to win only through massive numerical superiority. There are several reasons for this belief. Many of the western accounts are from German memoirs, some of which are self-serving. In the early part of the war, weakened by Stalin's purges and plagued by the inefficiencies and corruption of the Soviet state, many Soviet units did perform poorly. Accounts from the Soviet point of view, which can also sometimes be biased, were largely missing until after the Cold War, when a few began to trickle westward.

This stereotype fails to account for the gradual improvement of Soviet forces over the course of the conflict. War is a cruel classroom, and the Soviets learned their lessons as well as any. By the end of the war, they were capable of large-scale combined arms operations,

performing them skilfully over the last year of the war. At the tactical level, Soviet tank crews used terrain, weather and battlefield conditions to outmanoeuvre and defeat their German opponents, also using the characteristics of their weapons and equipment to full advantage.

Examples of Soviet skill in armoured warfare come to modern readers through the memoirs of Dmitriy Loza. He served as a tank officer in both

staff and command positions in the 46th Guards Tank Brigade of the 9th Guards Mechanised Corps during the last year of the war. His memoirs are more interesting because his unit used American M4 tanks delivered through Lend-Lease. There are few accounts of Soviet experiences with foreign-built armour available.

The United States delivered other light and medium tanks, such as the M-3 light and M3 medium tanks earlier in the war, but the Soviets complained that US tanks caught fire very easily when hit in the side or rear, even called the M3 medium a 'grave for seven brothers,' referring to the 7-man crew. To help solve this problem, the US sent M4A2 Shermans, fitted with twin diesel engines. Loza's unit used the M4A2, fitted with the long 76mm cannon. They called their new tank '*Emchas*,' a contraction of *M chetyre*, Russian for M4. The crewmen were *Emchisti*.

Soviet tank crews familiarised with the *Emcha* by completely disassembling one tank and putting it back together in working order. The brigade even had an American technical representative from the factory to advise them. The Soviet troops called him 'Misha.' They found that while the Sherman was top heavy and sometimes prone to overturning, it had good 'flotation,' able to cross soft or muddy terrain most other tanks could not. They also discovered American factory workers sometimes cleverly hid bottles of whiskey in the tanks for their Soviet allies to find.

ABOVE: A Tiger II of the German Heavy Tank Battalion 503 in Budapest, October 1944. The tank's ridged exterior is called *zimmerit* and was applied to reduce the adherence of magnetic mines. (BUNDESARCHIV)

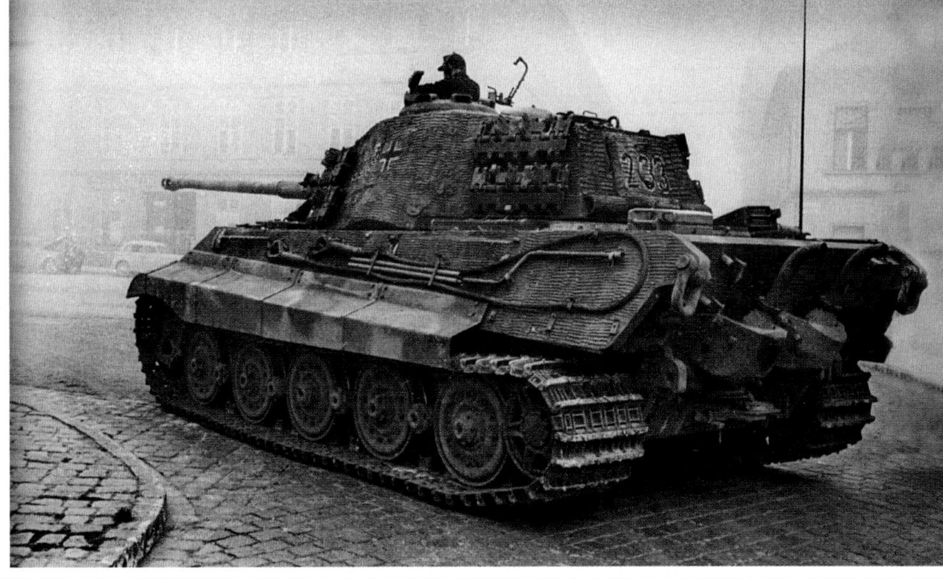

The Soviets developed tactics to deal with the more heavily armed and armoured German Tigers and Panthers. One group of Shermans would engage the panzers to draw their attention while another group manoeuvred to attack the enemy's flank, where the armour was thinner. The Soviets called this 'hunting with Borzois;' the tactic was similar to the western concept of 'fix and flank.' When German tanks were moving, the Soviet paired two Shermans against each panzer. The first Sherman fired an armour-piercing round at one of the panzer's tracks; a solid hit would break the track, causing the tank to slew around on its remaining, intact track. This would expose the panzer's side armour to the second Sherman, which would aim for the fuel tank. This tactic required the enemy tank to be within 500 metres, otherwise the shot would not break the track.

Loza also described an attack during a snowstorm on a German armoured position near Lysyanka, south of Kiev in Ukraine. A German infantry battalion with five Tiger tanks defended the area (like American soldiers, the Soviets apparently often identified any German tank as a Tiger). Attacking the Germans using the road would result in heavy losses, so the Soviets devised a different plan.

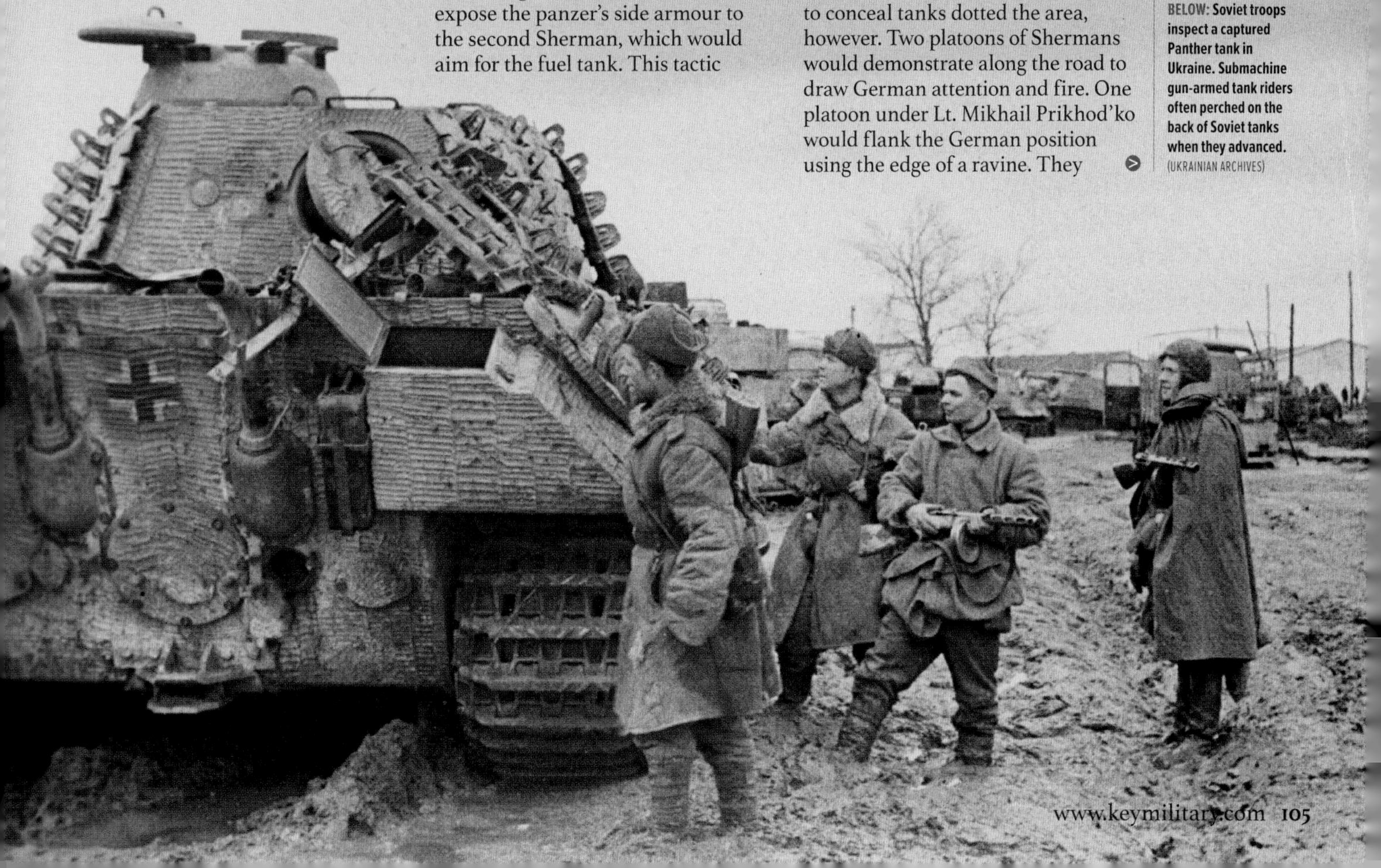

It appeared the Germans did not consider the snow-covered terrain passable by tanks, so their defences concentrated around the road. Several ravines large enough to conceal tanks dotted the area, however. Two platoons of Shermans would demonstrate along the road to draw German attention and fire. One platoon under Lt. Mikhail Prikhod'ko would flank the German position using the edge of a ravine. They

BELOW: Soviet troops inspect a captured Panther tank in Ukraine. Submachine gun-armed tank riders often perched on the back of Soviet tanks when they advanced. (UKRAINIAN ARCHIVES)

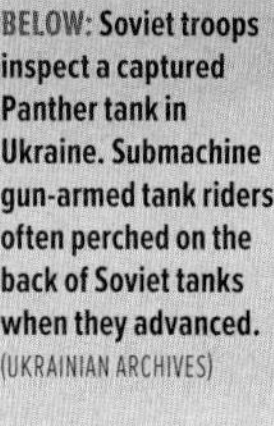

RIGHT: Shermans of the 9th Guards Mechanised Corps on the road to Vienna in March 1945. Each tank has a squad of infantry aboard. In combat, they supported one another as an effective tank-infantry team. (USAMHI)

felt the plan would work because the snow fell heavily, reducing visibility. A wind also blew directly against the advancing Soviets. While this was uncomfortable for the tank crews, the wind was blowing away from the Germans and so would mask the noise of the Sherman's engines. To further reduce noise, each Sherman ran on only one engine near idle.

The two groups coordinated their actions via radio. Prikhod'ko's tanks found a German outpost but surprised and captured the sentries. As they neared the main German position, the weather momentarily cleared, revealing two panzers only 70 metres away. Two Shermans fired armour-piercing rounds into the enemy tanks until both burned. The crews bailed out, but the Soviet tankers cut them down with machine gun fire. Now under fire from two directions, the Germans withdrew.

The 46th Guards Tank Brigade participated in the Soviet advance into Hungary and Austria in the final months of the war in Europe. On 9 April 1945, Loza, commanding the brigade's 1st battalion, led a raid into the heart of Vienna to seize key buildings ahead of the main advance. This included the parliament building, art museum, opera house and Academy of Sciences. His battalion had 18 operational Shermans (a full-strength battalion had 21), reinforced by a trio of SU-152 assault guns and a company of paratroopers acting as *tankodesantniki*, or 'tank riders.'

The task force succeeded in finding its way into the heart of Vienna, at one point driving down streets packed with civilians who didn't immediately realise the tanks were Soviet. Once they did, a response began to organise. Reaching their objective, Loza deployed his tanks and paratroopers into a perimeter with interlocking fields of fire, with the assault guns in reserve.

Soon German troops infiltrated into the area, dropping explosives on the *Emchas*. Most of the Sherman crews soon found arches or other covered areas to shelter under. At 0200 AM, the Germans cut the electricity. Their next attack came at dawn, but the Soviets expected such a move and were ready. Overnight the Germans manhandled an anti-tank gun onto the upper floor of a house and began firing. Loza sent one of the assault guns to deal with it. A single heavy 152mm round destroyed the gun and the house.

Next, several Panther tanks approached, each down a different street. Infantry sheltered behind each tank as it took position. The Shermans could not penetrate the Panther's frontal armour at that distance, so the Soviet tanks fell back into concealed positions and waited for opportunities for flank shots. One Sherman was hit

BELOW: Soviet troops atop their M4A2 Sherman in the final days of the war in Europe. The diesel-engined M4A2 served effectively in the Red Army. (US NATIONAL ARCHIVES)

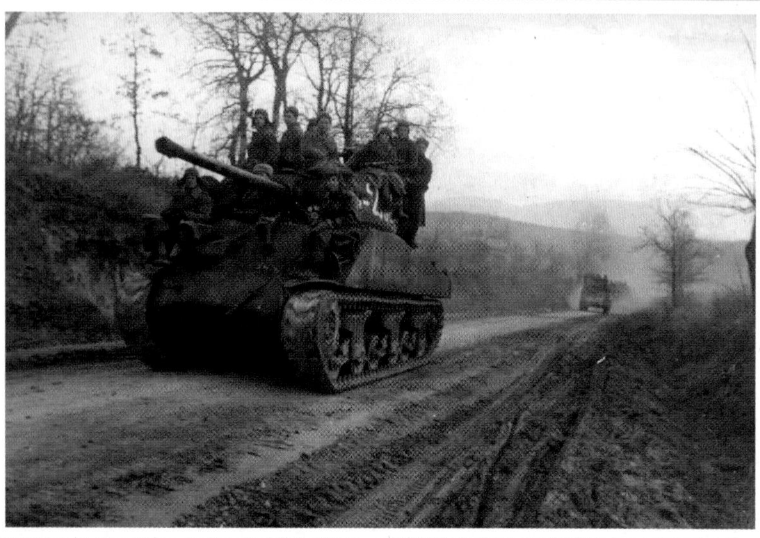

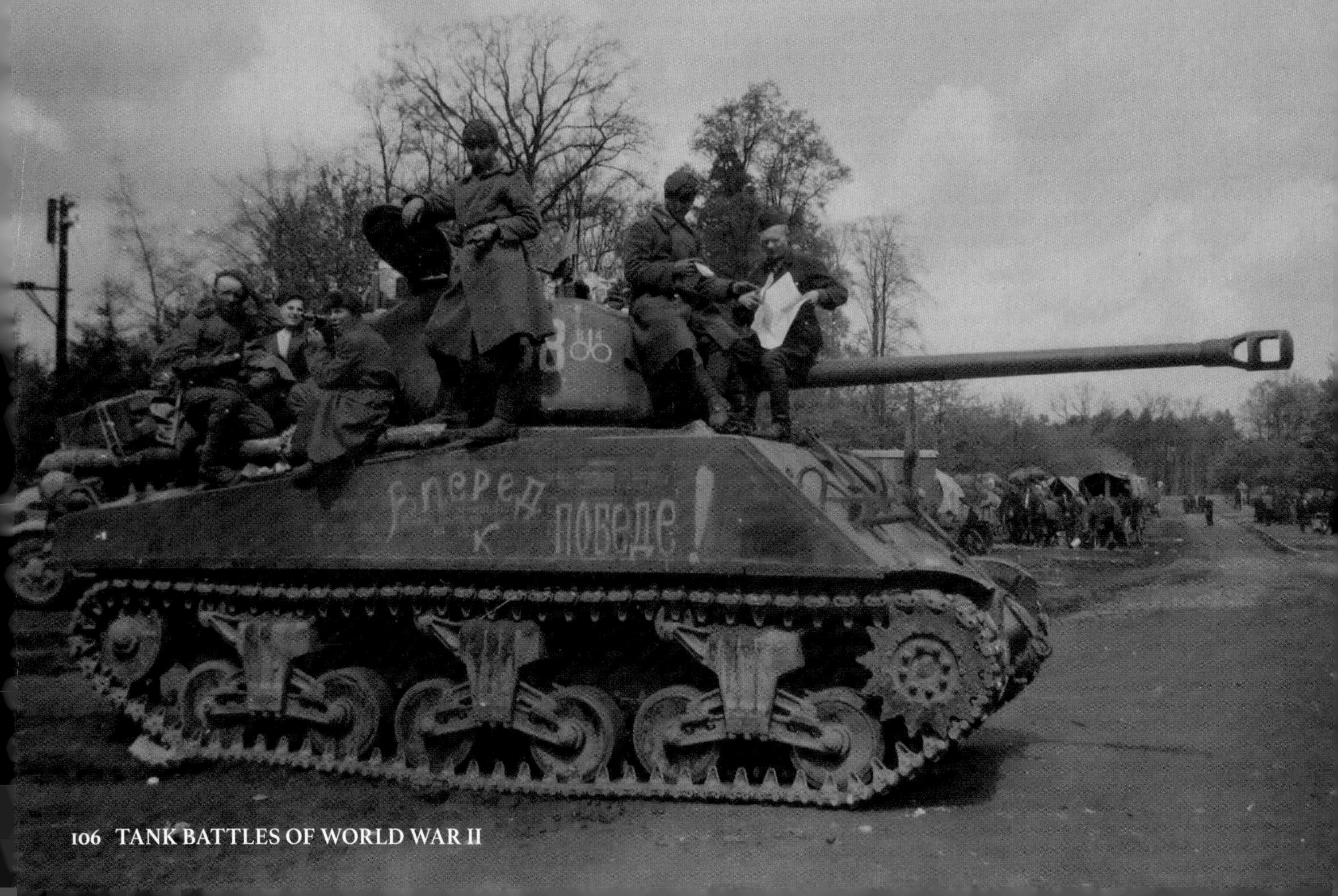

and immobilised, but the crew used smoke pots to obscure their location. Another Sherman soon towed it out of the line of fire.

Two Panthers and a platoon of infantry attacked a pair of Shermans. One Soviet gunner fired high-explosive rounds at the closing infantry, forcing them back. The Panthers hit the other *Emcha*, but were hit in return, one of them taking a track hit which left it sideways in the street. The battle became a cat and mouse game between the opposing tanks. Loza received periodic reports from his brigade commander, so he knew help was getting closer, he just had to hold out.

Loza again deployed his assault guns, this time against the Panthers. The *Emchas* laid down covering fire as the SU-152s got into position. As the firefight continued against the advancing Germans, one SU-152 fired a high-explosive round set with a concrete-piercing fuse at the Panther, knocking its turret completely off. The spectacle sapped German morale and they fell back.

Another attack came that afternoon, but the Soviets beat it back as well. In the evening of April 10, the rest of the 9th Guards Mechanised Corps arrived, relieving Loza and his task force. Their casualties proved surprisingly light: ten killed, fifteen wounded and four tanks lost. For his leadership, Loza was made a Hero of the Soviet Union, the highest decoration a Soviet soldier could receive. He later led his unit against the Japanese in Manchuria in August-September 1945. He retired from the Soviet Army as a colonel.

ABOVE: An M4A2 sits next to a ruined building in Vienna. During the fighting for the city the Soviets used large calibre artillery in a direct fire role to destroy German strongpoints. (US NATIONAL ARCHIVES)

LEFT: SS troops crowd atop a StuG in December 1944. As the Soviets advanced into Hungary and Austria, SS units fought bitter defensive actions against them. (POLISH ARCHIVES)

Pershing versus Panther

RIGHT: Tanks and infantry had to protect each other during urban fighting. Here, an infantryman with a Browning Automatic Rifle guides a T26E3 Pershing. Except for the commander, the rest of the crew is 'buttoned up,' ready for action. (US NATIONAL ARCHIVES)

BELOW: A combat cameraman poses in front of the 'Cologne Panther,' as it came to be known. The engagement is one of only a few to be filmed as it occurred. Note the 90mm shell hole in the side armour. (US NATIONAL ARCHIVES)

For most of the war, American tank crews used the M4 Sherman as their primary battle tank. In 1942, the Sherman ranked among the world's best tanks. By 1945, its shortcomings in firepower and armour protection showed. The US Army's answer to this dilemma was the T26E3, soon standardised as the M26 Pershing. The Pershing carried a 90mm cannon and better armour than the Sherman, making it roughly equivalent to a German Tiger I, though more reliable and easier to maintain.

In February 1945, the US Army sent 20 Pershings to Europe for field testing. Ten went to the US 3rd Armored Division, which gave one to the best tank crews in 10 of its tank companies. Staff Sgt. Robert Earley of 2nd Platoon, E Company, 32nd Armored Regiment, received a T26E3 at Stolberg, just east of Aachen. Earley had never lost a tank under his command; his new tank bore the designation 'E7' on its fender.

Cpl. Clarence Smoyer sat in the gunner's seat. Given a few rounds for practice, Smoyer aimed at a chimney on a farmhouse 1,200m away. The division commander, Maj. Gen. Maurice Rose, stood a few feet away, eager to observe the new tank's firepower. This made Smoyer nervous, but there was nothing to do except fire and hope the gun met expectations.

He pulled the trigger; muzzle flash blinded him, the noise deafened him and the muzzle blast knocked Rose off his feet. The chimney exploded in a shower of burst bricks. Smoyer went on to hit two more chimneys 1,500m away. Even the mud-spattered Gen. Rose applauded. Smoyer told his fellow crewmen, "The army needs to rush a whole bunch of these over here."

Within a few days Earley and Smoyer took their new tank into

combat. E Company attacked the town of Blatzheim around 23 February. Second Platoon took fire as they approached the town. One Sherman took a disabling hit and a second threw a track. Another Sherman became stuck in a crater, leaving only one Sherman and the Pershing operational. Suddenly a green tracer, the calling card of a German gun, slammed into the Sherman's turret, leaving Earley's crew alone.

Smoyer spotted the gun and Earley ordered the tank to stop so the gunner could fire accurately. Cpl. John DeRiggi, the loader, pushed a white phosphorus round into the breech of the 90mm. German shells hit the ground around the Pershing as Smoyer aimed and fired. His shot shattered a tree and started a fire around an 88mm gun. The driver reversed as DeRiggi reloaded; a German round struck the earth where they had just been. Smoyer's second shot hit another tree, surrounding another 88 in flames. Smoyer next destroyed some German entrenchments, the tank moving between shots.

Six Shermans from E Company arrived and all seven tanks entered Blatzheim. Afterward a few Sherman tankers joked about the Pershing being slow to reach the town – its cross-country speed was lower than a Sherman's. Smoyer replied, "I never saw any of you try to pass us." No one had a reply.

On the night of 3-4 March, 3rd Armored Division reached the outskirts of Cologne, a 2,000 year-old city straddling the Rhine. The twin spires of its cathedral remained standing despite RAF bombing three days earlier. Infantry led the way into the city with tanks in support. The Pershing acted as the lead tank, a dubious honour after the performance of crew and tank at Blatzheim. It's thicker armour and powerful armament gave it the best chance.

Each tank had a coloured panel on the engine deck to identify it to marauding Allied fighter-bombers. Tension held the crew; any window or doorway could conceal a German with a panzerfaust. Searching for targets through his gunsight, Smoyer spotted a glint of reflected light from a clock tower nearly a mile away. Concerned it might be an enemy artillery observer, he put a high-explosive round into the tower, collapsing it.

The next morning, Earley's tank again led the way, three Shermans behind it and infantry alongside. As they approached the cathedral, unknown to them a few Panzer IV and Panther tanks hid around it. An intact bridge over the Rhine lay just beyond the cathedral. The American leadership wanted that bridge; the tank crews sent to take it thought it was a suicide mission.

The American column crept toward the bridge, fighting as they went. At 1 PM, a large explosion shook the area, a column of smoke rising into the air. The Germans blew the bridge, giving the American soldiers a reprieve. Minutes later, their hopes were dashed when an order arrived to continue advancing.

The Pershing reached an intersection and stopped in some shadows. Suddenly a German tank appeared to their left. Smoyer traversed his turret, but the Panzer IV backed behind a building before he could target it. A few minutes later, Smoyer fired a round into the building concealing the enemy tank, partly collapsing it. That gave him an idea, so he put several more rounds into the structure until it collapsed onto the panzer, jamming its turret. Half the crew abandoned it while the rest drove the tank away. It was not seen again.

On a nearby street, Sherman tanks from F Company advanced toward the cathedral. A green tracer slammed into the lead Sherman, commanded by Lt. Karl Kellner, followed by another seconds later. The pressure of the hits blew the Sherman's hatches open. Kellner lost his left leg at the knee. Shrapnel struck the gunner's legs. The driver backed the tank away, but a third hit blew apart the tank's right track. Still, the driver got the tank backed around a corner and out of the line of fire. Kellner climbed out of his hatch and fell onto the engine deck. A war correspondent who would become famous after the war, Sgt. Andy Rooney, ran over and helped Kellner off the tank, but the young officer died minutes later. The loader and driver also died.

Suddenly their attacker appeared, a Panther tank commanded by Oberleutnant Wilhelm Bartelborth. The Americans ran for cover, but one combat cameraman, Jim Bates, ran three hundred yards to the nearby Pershing and told Earley about the Panther. It seemed to be guarding the cathedral. Early left Smoyer in command and went with Bates to investigate. They snuck into a building overlooking the cathedral square and spotted the Panther. Earley decided to advance to the square and take the Panther in the flank.

He moved back to the Pershing, warning the Sherman crews to stay back. DeRiggi loaded an armour piercing round. Smoyer said he would aim for the hull to guarantee a hit. Earley told him, "Shoot wherever you want. He's just sitting there like he owns the place." The loader grabbed a second round for a fast reload as Smoyer traversed the turret to the right so he would be ready when the Pershing rounded the corner.

Earley gave the order to advance and driver William McVey drove to the intersection. Coming into it, they saw the Panther, its gun pointed right at them. The driver hit the gas and the Pershing jumped forward into the intersection, McVey hoping to get them out of the way. Smoyer saw the Panther through his sight, its gun pointed right at them.

The Germans didn't fire. Bartelborth had never seen a Pershing before and thought it might be a German tank, so he told his gunner to hold fire. It gave the Americans a precious few seconds. Smoyer did not hesitate. He fired, sending a round into the right side of the Panther. It tore through the armour and into the panzer's engine compartment. The tank caught fire and Bartelborth leapt out of the commander's hatch and jumped to the ground on the tank's opposite side.

The firing raised a cloud of dust, so Smoyer could see only the outline of the Panther. DeRiggi reloaded and Smoyer fired again. The second round pierced the Panther's armour with a shower of sparks and entered the crew compartment, starting another fire. Two more Germans came out of the tank, one with his clothes on fire. Taking no chances,

Smoyer put a third round into the German tank, completing its destruction. Earley ordered the Pershing back around the corner. The crew collectively realised their luck – they had survived. Around the corner the Panther's ammunition cooked off.

Jim Bates managed to film the entire fight and took footage of the crew as well. A few minutes later the Pershing and its crew were back in the war. The duel became famous, largely because it was filmed; the video can easily be found online today. In 1945, that film went back to America to be shown in newsreels at cinemas. Played in his hometown, Smoyer's sister-in-law saw him on the screen. She convinced the theatre's owner to replay the film for Smoyer's parents, who had never been to a cinema, so they could see their son was still alive.

LEFT: The twin spires of Cologne cathedral are visible over the barrel of the Pershing's main gun. (US NATIONAL ARCHIVES)

BELOW: Sgt. Earley's Pershing tank on a street in Cologne. Note the .50-calibre machine gun atop the turret is covered by a tarp, indicating the crew doesn't plan to expose themselves to use it. (US NATIONAL ARCHIVES)

Afterward

Lessons for the postwar world

RIGHT: Germany lay in ruins at the war's end. These American M4 Shermans move along a cleared street in Muenster, April 1945. The sandbags on their front armour are meant to protect against panzerfausts. (US NATIONAL ARCHIVES)

Armoured warfare reached its greatest heights in World War Two. In terms of sheer numbers and scale of operations, few tank actions since have come close. The tank cemented its place as a primary weapon system for any modern army. It retains that place to this day, despite the rise of new threats.

In the immediate aftermath of the war, the former battlefields were still littered with the hulks of destroyed tanks. It took years, sometimes decades, to clear them all. Many went to the scrapyard or were recycled for their metal. Others were sold or given to armies around the world as military aid. National armies kept the newest and best models in inventory. Today they can be seen in museums and a few private collections, where they are occasionally brought out for reenactments and shows. Even eight decades after the war, one is occasionally found in a bog or lake and recovered.

The Allied armies took examples of the latest German tanks, such as the Tiger II, for testing. Soviet tank development continued, while in the West most weapons development stagnated for several years after the war due to the general demobilisation. Research soon resumed as the Cold War brought new tensions.

Tanks grew rapidly in size and capability after the war. A tanks arms race began in 1941 on the Eastern Front between Germany and the Soviet Union. Each nation produced bigger tanks with larger main guns and thicker armour in an effort to create a superior fighting vehicle, looking for a decisive advantage over their opponent. The race spread to the Western Allies from late 1943 on. After the war this race continued between East and West. Late war designs such as the British Centurion, American M26 Pershing and Soviet T-44 began the Cold War tank race, eventually leading to the modern Challenger, M1 Abrams and Russian T-90.

BELOW: These captured tanks sit at the Henschel testing ground in Germany soon after the war's end. From the left, a Panther, Tiger II, Jagdtiger tank destroyer and another Tiger II with a destroyed barrel. (US NATIONAL ARCHIVES)

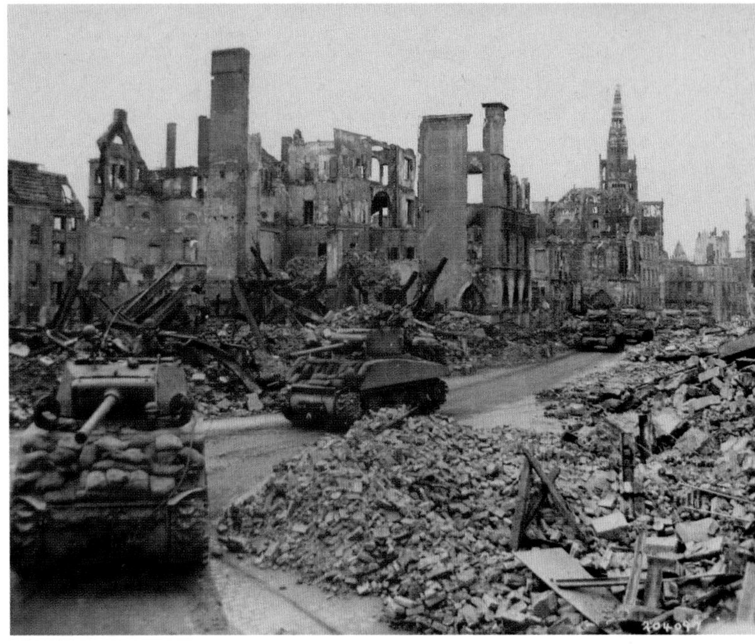

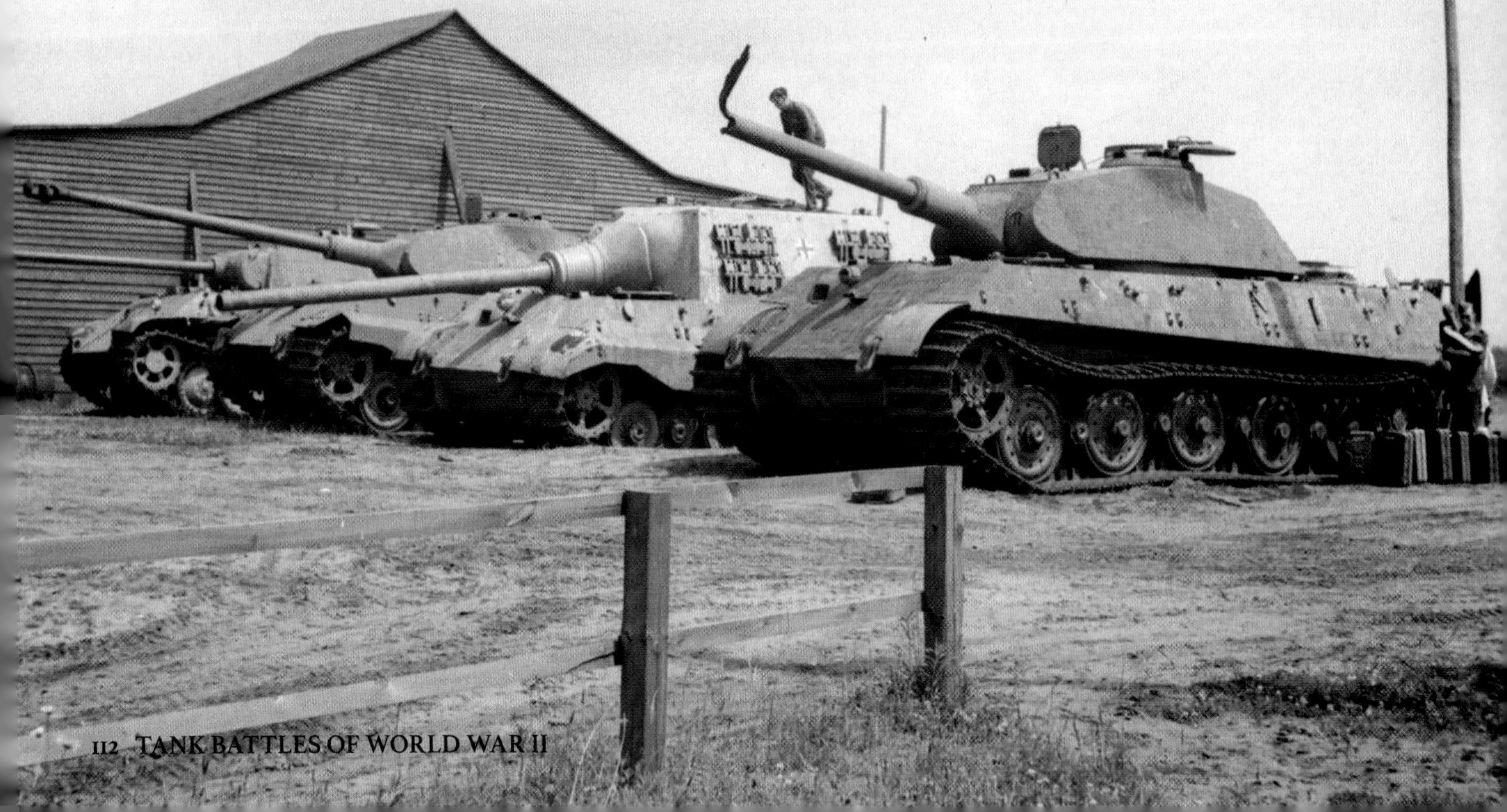

Tanks saw wide use in the Cold War, notably during the Arab-Israeli and Indo-Pakistani conflicts. Even wars in places thought unsuitable for tanks saw their use. During the Vietnam War, North and South Vietnamese, American and Australian Forces all used armoured vehicles to good effect despite predictions they would not perform well in jungle areas. When North Vietnam invaded the South in 1972 and 1975, they did so not with irregular guerrillas, but with tank-heavy combined arms armies. In 1975 the North invaded with at least 1,200 tanks, more than the British Army employed during Operation Goodwood in 1944. South Vietnam ended as a nation when two

North Vietnamese tanks, a Soviet T-54 and Chinese Type 59, crashed through the gate of the Independence Palace in 1975.

Tanks show no sign of leaving the battlefield. The rise of anti-tank guided missiles in the 1960s through early 1970s and the proliferation of drones in the 21st Century both caused pundits to claim the tank as obsolete. Innovation and new technologies have kept tanks on the battlefield in large numbers, however. Modern tanks are in every respect more capable and liberally equipped with electronic systems and features a World War Two tank crew would envy. Even so, today's armour draws a direct line to their World War Two forebearers.

ABOVE: In the final days of the war, Germany had to improvise weapons. This Tiger II turret is mounted on a railroad car. (US NATIONAL ARCHIVES)

LEFT: Appearing just too late to see action in World War II, the British Centurion tank served well throughout the Cold War, seeing several upgrades. This is a Canadian example in 1963. (LIBRARY AND ARCHIVES CANADA)

LEFT: American tanks saw action again in Korea in 1950. This US Marine Corps M26 Pershing is providing overwatch as North Korean prisoners are rounded up in Seoul. (US NAVY)

Glossary and Terms

The language of armoured warfare

AB	Armoured Brigade
AD	Armoured Division
AP	Armour-Piercing
APCR	Armour Piercing Composite Rigid, a type of cannon ammunition
AT	Anti-Tank
Bazooka	A US handheld anti-tank rocket launcher.
BEF	British Expeditionary Force, the British military force which went to France in 1940.
CC	Combat Command, usually designated A, B or R for Reserve, part of the US Army's Armoured Division organisation of September 1943.
DCM	Distinguished Conduct Medal
DLM	*Division Légère Mécanique*, French for 'Light Mechanised Division,' and early war French armoured unit.
FOO	Forward Observation Officer
GTA	Guards Tank Army. Red Army units which performed well in battle could be awarded the status of a Guards formation.
HE	High Explosive
ID	Infantry Division
KwK	*KampfwagenKanone*, German for 'armoured fighting vehicle cannon'
PaK	*PanzerabwehrKanone*, German for anti-tank gun.
Panzerfaust	'Armour Fist,' a German handheld disposable anti-tank weapon.
Panzerschreck	'Armour Terror,' a German handheld reloadable anti-tank weapon, copied from examples of the American bazooka, captured in North Africa in 1942-43.
PB	Panzer Brigade
PIAT	Projector, Infantry, Anti-Tank, UK infantry AT weapon
RB	Rifle Brigade
RTR	Royal Tank Regiment
Tank destroyer	US term for a self-propelled anti-tank gun.
WDF	Western Desert Force

BELOW: Cromwell and Challenger tanks at the British victory parade in Berlin, July 1945. (LIBRARY AND ARCHIVES CANADA)